YOU CAN COOK FOR

(OR EVEN TWO)

YOU CAN COOK FOR

(OR EVEN TWO)

by Louise Pickoff

GRAMERCY PUBLISHING COMPANY • NEW YORK

This edition published by Gramercy Publishing Company,
a division of Crown Publishers, Inc.,
by arrangement with A. S. Barnes and Company, Inc.
f g h

In Memory of My Father
Harry Pickoff

acknowledgments

To the inspiration of Mary Land, who wrote "Louisiana Cookery." When she lived in Corpus Christi, Texas, for a short time, Mrs. Land encouraged me to write this book.

And, of course, the influence of my mother, Mrs. Harry Pickoff, who is the best cook in Taylor, Texas.

Then to my business partner, Mrs. Martha Mahurin Dahlberg, who so kindly has been doing some of my share of work while I have been pounding the typewriter during office hours.

And my appreciation to Central Power and Light Company, Corpus Christi, Texas, which provided its recipe files; and to the Corpus Christi *Caller-Times* Food Department.

Dedicated
to Those Who Cook for One
Like It or Not!

contents

introduction

Some of my married friends and acquaintances thought I was crazy when I told them I was compiling a cookbook for one person. The response was generally the same, "Now, Louise, you really don't cook meals just for yourself. You just open cans and stand in the kitchen and eat. Why if I lived alone I would starve before I would cook a meal. When John . . . or Joe . . . (or whatever the name) . . . is out of town I just nibble or go out and eat."

But, fortunately, I was soon encouraged. I started telling single men and women about my book, and they were very enthusiastic. They said they would eat at home more if they could find a complete cookbook for one person. That is why I have tried to put everything but the kitchen sink into this book.

Everybody has a hobby. With shorter working hours there is more free time. In fact, some people have several hobbies. There are swimming and tennis. Bridge and poker. Golf and fishing . . . reading . . . playing chess . . . watching TV . . . collecting . . . building furniture . . . hunting . . . and if you are like me . . . one of your hobbies is cooking.

I don't know of a more relaxing way to end any kind of day . . . working or loafing . . . than to turn on the TV . . . read the paper . . . imbibe of your favorite after-five refreshment . . . and cook all at the same time. It can be done because I do it. Most of the recipes in this book are easily prepared, and once the ingredients have been put together they do not call for constant watching. Too, most of these preparations can be completely cooked, left to stand, and reheated when you get ready to serve. It will be a great help to you if you don't like to eat until you are really hungry.

When cooking for one, we are too prone to prepare the same type of meals, day after day, week after week. You don't want to wear the same dress—or the same suit—day after day, week after week, so why eat the same food! The next time you go grocery shopping, make yourself try out something new. In order to vary my meals, I find a safe, practical way is to buy food items that are on special that day. If I make a bad buy, it won't wreck my budget too much . . . but if it is a good buy, I have made a new cooking friend.

As to breakfasts. Why not start the day with some variety? As for myself, I must have an egg, bacon, two slices of toast, and coffee, when I am working. If I didn't eat a substantial breakfast, no one could stand to be around me until lunch time. But in order to vary, I prepare my eggs differently every morning. You will find all of these recipes in this cookbook. If you just eat dry cereals with cream, buy assorted kinds. Add different fruits each morning. But be sure to eat enough of something so that you can be pleasant or at least withstand the morning hours.

One advantage of eating alone is that you can wear what you want and you can eat what you want.

Quite often people ask me if I set my table attractively with flowers and candles. I must admit the answer is no. I live in an efficiency apartment and I eat off the coffee table in the living room. I either put my china on a tray or a place mat. I use chip-free china, and I use silver that I have not used while cooking. In order to save on laundry

I use paper napkins. After watching the commercials on TV. doesn't everybody?

I refuse to comment on my table manners while eating alone. Just use your imagination!

So, here's to fun when cooking for one (or even two)!

English Equivalent

Measures

	American	English
1 cup of breadcrumbs (fresh)	1½ oz.	3 oz.
1 cup of flour or other powdered grains	4 ·oz.	5 oz.
1 cup of sugar	7 oz.	8 oz.
1 cup of icing sugar	4½ oz.	5 oz.
1 cup of butter or other fats	8 oz.	8 oz.
1 cup of raisins, etc.	5 oz.	6 oz.
1 cup of grated cheese	4 oz.	4 oz.
1 cup of syrup, etc.	12 oz.	14 oz.

1 English pint	20 fluid ounces
1 American pint	16 fluid ounces
1 American cup	8 fluid ounces
8 American tablespoons	4 fluid ounces
1 American tablespoon	½ fluid ounce
3 American teaspoons	½ fluid ounce
1 English tablespoon	⅔ to 1 fluid ounce (approx.)
1 English tablespoon	4 teaspoons

The American measuring tablespoon holds ¼ oz. flour.

HERBS

Herbs are used so often these days that no cookbook is complete without an herb chart. Do use them sparingly until you have learned their full strength. Also, don't use herbs in every dish as it will make your food too monotonous.

When using in stews, soups, and sauces, add herbs within the last hour of cooking.

Uncooked mixtures, such as fruit and vegetable juices, should have plenty of time to let the flavors mingle when adding herbs. It is suggested that in this instance you add herbs about 24 hours ahead of time.

When preparing dishes for one, use about 1/8 teaspoon of herbs.

HERB CHART Epicurean seasoning requires delicate flavors. Use herbs lightly and to taste.

	BASIL	BAY	MARJORAM	OREGANO	PARSLEY	ROSEMARY	SAFFRON	SAGE	SAVORY	TARRAGON	THYME
Appetizers	Tomato Juice Seafood Cocktail	Tomato Juice Aspic	Liver Pate Stuffed Mushrooms Butters	Guacamole Tomato	Garnish	Fruit Cup	Saffron Butter	Cottage Cheese Cheddar Spread	Vegetable Juice Cocktail	Ravigote Butter Fish Cocktail Tomato Juice	Tomato Juice Fish Cocktails
Soups	Tomato Turtle Spinach Minestrone	Stock Herb Bouquet	Spinach Clam Bouillon Mock Turtle Onion	Tomato Bean Minestrone	Any Garnish Herb Bouquet	Turtle Pea Spinach Chicken	Bouillabaisse Fish Consomme Chicken	Cream Soup Chowders	Fish Consomme Lentil Bean	Consomme Chicken Mushroom Tomato	Borscht Gumbo, Pea Clam Chowder Vegetable
Fish	Shrimp Broiled Fish Filet of Sole Mackerel	Court Bouillon Pickled Fish Fish Kebab	Broiled Fish Baked Fish Creamed Fish	Stuffing	Any Court Bouillon	Salmon Stuffing	Halibut Sole	Stuffings	Broiled Fish Baked Fish	Broiled Fish Lobster Thermador	Broiled Fish Baked Fish Fried Fish
Eggs or Cheese	Scrambled Eggs Cream Cheese Welsh Rarebit		Omelette Aux Fines Herbes Scrambled Eggs	Huevos Rancheros Boiled Eggs	Omelette Creamed Eggs Scrambled Eggs	Omelette Scrambled Eggs	Cream Cheese Scrambled Eggs	Cheddar Cottage	Scrambled Eggs Deviled Eggs	All egg Dishes Omelette Aux Fines Herbes	Shirred Eggs Cottage Cheese
Meats	Liver Lamb Sausage	Stews Pot Roast Swiss Kebab Tripe	Pot Roast Pork Beef Veal	Pork Sausage Lamb Meat Loaf	Lamb Veal Steak Stews	Lamb Veal Ragout Beef Stews Ham Loaf	Veal	Stews Pork Sausage	Pork Veal	Veal Sweet-breads Yorkshire Pudding	Mutton Meat Loaf Veal
Poultry and Game	Venison Duck	Fricasee Stews	Creamed Chicken Stuffings Goose	Marinades Stuffings Pheasant Guinea Hen	Stuffings Herb Bouquets	Partridge Capon Duck Rabbit	Arroz Con Pollo Chicken	Goose Turkey Rabbit Stuffings	Chicken Stuffings	Chicken Squab Duck	Stuffings Venison Fricassee Jugged Hare
Vegetables	Egg Plant Squash Tomatoes Onions	Boiled Potatoes Carrots Stewed Tomatoes	Carrots Zucchini Peas Spinach	Tomatoes Cabbage Lentils Broccoli	Potatoes Carrots Peas	Peas Spinach French Fried Potatoes	Risotto Spanish Rice Rice	Lima Beans Egg Plant Onions Tomatoes	Beans Rice Lentils Sauerkraut	Salsify Celery Root Mushrooms Baked Potatoes	Onions Carrots Beets
Salads	Tomato Mixed Green Sea Food	Fish Salads Aspic	Chicken Mixed Green	Tomato Aspic Fish Salad	Potato Fish Mixed Green	Fruit	Fish		Mixed Green String Bean Russian	Mixed Green Chicken Fish	Pickled Beets Tomato Aspics

YOU CAN COOK FOR 1

(OR EVEN TWO)

suggested kitchen equipment

Your kitchen should be one of the most important rooms in your apartment or house. It is suggested that when you find you are not using certain kitchen equipment, give it away— don't clutter up your kitchen. If you are starting with limited equipment my mottto is: "Take anything anybody will give you." You might find a use for it later, or it may give you an impetus to try out new recipes.

The ideal kitchen should have the following:

For measuring:

Set measuring spoons
Set dry measuring cups
Set liquid measuring cups
Pint and quart measures

Spatulas:

Rubber spatula. Sometimes called rubber plate and bowl scraper.
Straight metal spatula. This can be so designed to serve also as a pancake turner.

Flexible spatulas. Large and small for removing cakes from pan. Can also be used in icing cakes.

Knives, forks, and spoons:

Long slicer, for roasts
Two or three sharp paring knives. Best your budget will afford.
Bread knife with saw tooth edge. For bread, cakes, etc.
Knife to use with chopping bowl
Grapefruit knife
Kitchen fork and knife. Can serve as carving set.
Long handled fork
Long handled spoon
Wooden spoon
Several tablespoons
Large spoons with holes or slots

To mix things with:

Flat wire whip
Pastry blender
Hand mixer or rotary egg beater. Electric big mixer if you have room and can afford it.

To work with vegetables, meats and fruits:

Vegetable parer. A must! Available at variety store.
Set of graters
Lemon squeezer
Small ball cutter
Apple corer
Strawberry huller
Shrimp deveiner

Brushes:

Pastry brush

Vegetable brush
Bottle brush

To open things:

Can opener. New electric ones are wonderful.
Jar opener
Bottle opener
Corkscrew. Can usually be found with hand can opener.

Bowls:

Chopping bowl
Mixing bowls. Recommend the new lightweight plastic
bowls with lip for pouring.

Sauce pans, kettle and skillets:

3 sauce pans, 2 to 4 quart sizes, with covers
Double boiler, if you do not have an electric range
Large kettle with steamer and basket for deep fat frying.
Electric ones are preferred as you can adjust the temperature needed.
3 skillets. Two cast iron or cast aluminum. One 9 to 10
inch size. The other 6 to 7 inch. One 3 inch is very useful
for melting butter or making small portions of sauce.
Electric skillet. Of course, this is not a must, but if you
have ever used one you will never do without it again.

Baking pans:

1 square baking pan, 9 inches square and 2 inches deep
2 round layer pans, 8 inch diameter and at least 1¼ inches
deep
2 round layer pans, 9 inch diameter and at least 1½ inches
deep
1 oblong pan, 13 inches by 9 inches and 2 inches deep

1 pie pan, 8 or 9 inches in diameter and at least 1¼ inches deep
1 loaf pan, 9 by 5 inches and 3 inches deep
1 cookie sheet, without sides
1 jelly roll pan or baking sheet with low sides, 15½ inches by 10½ inches, ½ inch deep
1 muffin pan
1 cornbread stick pan

Roasting pan:

Roasting pan with rack. This is for the time you are going to have dinner guests and you want to prepare your favorite roast or bake poultry.

Strainers:

Wire strainers. Suggest fine, very fine, and coarse
Colander
Flour sifter

Pastry extras:

Pastry set. Or, you can use wax paper.
Pastry fluter. Or, you can use a fork.

Dough cutters:

Cutters of different sizes for biscuits, cookies, etc.

Molds:

Molds, plain and fancy . . . large and individual sizes
Ring mold
Set of custard cups

Boards:

Bread board
Wooden chopping board. This is a must!

Cheese board

Grinder:

Food grinder, with attachments

Slicers:

Cheese cutter
Egg slicer

Ice:

Ice crusher. Electric, of course. Or, wrap clean cloth
around ice and pound with hammer

*Some of the items below are a must—Others are just
nice to have around the kitchen:*

Rolling pin. Large wine bottle could be substituted.
Funnel
Tongs
Bottle stopper for the bottled carbonated drinks when you
use only a portion
Canister set
Bread box
Cake safe
Cookie jar
Set of refrigerator dishes with covers
Plastic refrigerator covers and bags
Waxed paper
Aluminum foil, for baking, for freezing, and for covering
Dish pan
Pot holders
Frozen food knife
Dish towels
Paper towels
Sponge or dish cloth

Soap
Steel wool
Cleaning powder
Knife sharpener
Garbage can. Electric disposal would be super!
Waste basket
Cook book—YOU CAN COOK FOR ONE (OR EVEN
  TWO) by Louise Pickoff, published by A. S. Barnes
  & Co.

helpful
charts
and tables

You can probably call me a "buff" on charts. Since I started collecting recipes, I collected charts. Like some people who collect stamps or coins, I am always excited when I find a chart that will make cooking easier. It saves time looking for information in a variety of books. Since I compiled this cookbook, I find that I seldom look elsewhere for reference. Here you will find the seven basic foods needed for a balanced diet; a table of divided measures; how to prepare macaroni, spaghetti, or noodles for one; an electric fry pan cooking chart; charts on herbs and spices; interesting information on the most popular cheeses and when to serve; and a wine chart which will help you to brighten the atmosphere while you dine.

7 BASIC FOODS NEEDED FOR EVERYDAY LIVING

Leafy, Green, and Yellow Vegetables
Citrus Fruits, Tomatoes, and Raw Cabbage
Potatoes, other Vegetables, and Fruit
Milk and Milk Products

Meat, Fish, Poultry, and Eggs
Bread and Cereal
Butter and Margarine

When cooking for one, the worst brain teaser seems to be dividing measurements to suit your needs. The table below should make cooking easier:

TABLE OF DIVIDED MEASURES

Speck	Less than ⅛ tsp.
⅓ or ¼ tsp........................	Pinch
⅓ or ½ tsp........................	Pinch
½ of ¼ tsp........................	⅛ tsp.
½ of ¾ tsp........................	⅜ tsp.
3 tsp.	1 TBS.
⅓ of 1 TBS........................	1 tsp.
⅓ of 2 TBS........................	2 tsp.
⅓ of 5 TBS........................	1 TBS. plus 2 tsp.
⅓ of 7 TBS........................	2 TBS. plus 1 tsp.
½ of 1 TBS........................	1½ tsp.
½ of 3 TBS........................	1 TBS. plus 1½ tsp.
½ of 5 TBS........................	2 TBS. plus 1½ tsp.
½ of 7 TBS........................	3 TBS. plus 1½ tsp.
2 TBS.	⅛ cup
4 TBS.	¼ cup
5 TBS. plus 1 tsp...	⅓ cup
8 TBS.	½ cup
10 TBS. plus 2 tsp.	⅔ cup
12 TBS.	¾ cup
16 TBS.	1 cup
⅓ of ¼ cup	1 TBS. plus 1 tsp.
⅓ of ⅓ cup	1 TBS. plus 2-⅓ tsp.
⅓ of ½ cup	2 TBS. plus 2 tsp.
⅓ of ⅔ cup	3 TBS. plus 1-⅔ tsp.
⅓ of ¾ cup	¼ cup
½ of ¼ cup	2 TBS.

½ of ⅓ cup	2 TBS. plus 2 tsp.
½ of ½ cup	¼ cup
½ of ⅔ cup	⅓ cup
½ of ¾ cup	6 TBS.
2 cups	1 pt.
2 pts.	1 qt.
1 qt.	4 cups
4 qts.	1 gal.
8 qts.	1 peck
4 pecks	1 bushel
16 oz. (dry measure)	1 lb.

TABLE OF MEASUREMENTS FOR MACARONI, SPAGHETTI, AND NOODLES

When cooking for one, it is rather futile to prepare a casserole dish. It doesn't keep too well as leftovers, and trying to "eat your way out of it" can become very tiring.

However, you can prepare macaroni, spaghetti, and noodles in small amounts. Using the measurements below, a small saucepan filled about three-quarters with water, and a half teaspoon salt, you can have a quick dish. Be sure to rinse macaroni, spaghetti, and noodles before mixing with anything else or serving.

4 oz. or 1 cup uncooked macaroni makes two cups
5 oz. or 1 cup uncooked spaghetti makes two cups
2½ oz. or 1 cup uncooked noodles makes 1¼ cups

Or: After rinsing macaroni, spaghetti, or noodles, add cooked meat or cheese Cover to melt cheese.
Or: See page 71 for Individual Meat and Noodles

ELECTRIC FRY PAN COOKING CHART

FOOD	TEMPERATURE	DIRECTIONS
Bacon	325°	Place overlapping bacon slices from package in cold fry pan. Set dial at 325° and while bacon heats, separate slices so they lie flat. Turn bacon as it browns. Fat may be spooned off as it accumulates. When bacon is crisp, remove and drain on paper towel.
Canadian Bacon	325°	Preheat fry pan at 325° until light blinks out. Melt 1 TBS. shortening. Fry Canadian bacon until lightly browned on both sides.
Cheese Sandwich	325°	Preheat fry pan at 325° until light blinks out. Place cheddar cheese between two slices of bread. Butter the outside of the sandwiches. Brown sandwiches on both sides.
Chicken	360°	Preheat fry pan at 360° until light blinks out. Dredge chicken in seasoned flour and brown in 1 cup shortening. Simmer covered at 225° for 25–30 minutes with ½ cup water.
Eggs, Fried	300°	Preheat fry pan at 300° until light blinks out. Add ½ TBS. butter or margarine for each egg to be fried. Break egg into a cup and slip carefully into the pan. Turn the egg over or cook covered, as preferred.

ELECTRIC FRY PAN COOKING CHART *(Continued)*

FOOD	TEMPERATURE	DIRECTIONS
Eggs, Poached	225°	Grease bottom of fry pan. Add 3 cups water, cover, and set at 225°. When light blinks out, slip eggs from a cup into the water. Cover and cook 2½ to 3 minutes. Remove eggs with slotted spoon.
Eggs, Scrambled	300°	Preheat fry pan at 300° until light blinks out. Mix 6 eggs, ½ tsp. salt, dash of pepper, and 6 TBS. milk or cream together with a fork. Melt 2 TBS. butter or margarine in pan. Add egg mixture and as it cooks, gently stir it from bottom. Do not stir constantly. Cook until set, but soft and moist.
Fish	350°	Wash fish, dry on paper towels. Dip fish in milk and roll in flour. Season. Place in refrigerator for one hour, in order that flour will cling to fish when fried. Preheat fry pan at 350° until light blinks out. Melt 1 cup shortening (or use cooking oil) in pan. Brown fish thoroughly on one side. Turn and brown on the other.
French Toast	325°	Preheat fry pan at 325° until light blinks out. With fork beat 1 egg, dash of salt, 1 tsp. sugar and 2 TBS. milk together lightly. Melt 2 TBS. butter or margarine in pan. Quickly dip 4 slices of day-old bread into egg mixture until coated, not soaked. Brown on both sides in hot butter. Serve with syrup, jelly, honey, applesauce, or confectioner's sugar. Cinnamon sugar can be substituted for 1 tsp. sugar.

ELECTRIC FRY PAN COOKING CHART (*Continued*)

FOOD	TEMPERATURE	DIRECTIONS
Ham	350°	Preheat fry pan at 350° until light blinks out. Rub a piece of ham fat over fry pan. Select tenderized ham or smoked picnic slices ¼″ to ¾″ thick. Slash edges to prevent curling. Brown well on both sides. Spoon off fat as it accumulates.
Hamburgers	350°	Preheat fry pan at 350° until light blinks out. Melt 2 TBS. shortening in pan. Fry hamburgers brown on one side. Turn and brown on the other.
Lamb Chops	350°	Preheat fry pan at 350° until light blinks out. Melt 1 TBS. shortening (or use cooking oil) in pan. Select chops ½″ to 1″ thick. Slash fat edge to prevent curling. Cook about 8 minutes on each side to desired degree of doneness. Spoon off fat as it accumulates during cooking. Tenderizer may be used if desired.
Liver	325°	Use liver cut in ¼″ slices. Remove outer membrane and vein and roll liver in seasoned flour. Fry bacon in fry pan. Remove bacon and fry liver at 325° about 5 minutes on each side.
Minute Steak	375°	Preheat fry pan at 375° until light blinks out. Melt 2 TBS. shortening (or use cooking oil) in pan. Brown steaks on one side. Turn and brown on the other.
Oysters, Fried	350°	Drain oysters. Dip in beaten egg, then in fine cracker crumbs. Allow oysters to dry about 10 minutes. Preheat fry pan to

ELECTRIC FRY PAN COOKING CHART (*Continued*)

FOOD	TEMPERATURE	DIRECTIONS
		350° until light blinks out. Melt ¼ cup shortening in pan (or use cooking oil). Fry the oysters on both sides until golden brown.
Pancakes	375°	Add 1 egg, 2 TBS. melted shortening or cooking oil, and 1 cup milk to each cup of pancake mix. Preheat fry pan at 375° until light blinks out. Bake pancakes.
Pork Chops	350°	Preheat fry pan at 350° until light blinks out. Melt 1 TBS. shortening (or cooking oil) in pan. Brown chops thoroughly on one side. Turn and brown on other. Add ¼ cup water. Cover and cook 10–15 minutes at 225°. If desired recrisp chops at 350° in uncovered pan.
Potatoes, Raw Fried or American Fried	350°	Cut peeled potatoes in slices ⅛″ thick. Preheat fry pan at 350° until light blinks out. Melt 3 TBS. shortening (or cooking oil) in pan. Place potatoes in pan and season with salt and pepper. Brown thoroughly on one side. Turn and brown on other side. Do not cover pan.
Round Steak	350°	Preheat fry pan at 350° until light blinks out. Melt 2 TBS. shortening (or use cooking oil) in pan. Dip thinly sliced round steak in seasoned flour and brown well on both sides. Add ¾ cup water. Cover and cook about 30 minutes at 225°. Or sprinkle tenderizer on steak one hour before frying. Fry in oiled pan 10–15 minutes until done.

ELECTRIC FRY PAN COOKING CHART (*Continued*)

FOOD	TEMPERATURE	DIRECTIONS
Sausage, Pork and Venison	325°	Place sausages in fry pan with ½ cup water. Set at 325°, cover and steam about 5 minutes. Drain. Remove cover and brown sausages.
Steak (all types)	350°	Preheat fry pan at 350° until light blinks out. Melt 1 TBS. shortening (or use cooking oil) in pan. Select steak ½″ to 1″ thick. Slash fat edges to prevent curling. Cook from 7 to 10 minutes on one side until blood comes to surface. Turn. Cook on other side until done. Or sprinkle tenderizer on steak one hour before frying.
Veal Chops	350°	Preheat fry pan at 350° until light blinks out. Melt 3 TBS. shortening (or use cooking oil) in pan. Dip chops in beaten egg, then in fine bread or cracker crumbs. Brown well on both sides. Add ¾ cup water, cover, and cook about 30 minutes at 225°. To recrisp, remove cover and brown at 350°. Or, sprinkle tenderizer on steak one hour before frying. Fry in oiled pan until chop is done.

LIST OF HERBS MOST OFTEN USED

BAY LEAVES—Flavor particularly good in practically all meat cooking; also in vegetable and meat soups and sauces.

CHERVIL—Flavor like parsley but milder. Young leaves may be used in meat and vegetable soups, salads, and as a garnish.

AROMATIC SEED CHART

	ANISE	CARAWAY	CARDAMON	CELERY	CORIANDER	CUMIN	DILL	FENNEL	MUSTARD	POPPY SEED	SESAME SEED
Appetizers	Crackers	Corn Crisps	Fruit Cup	Corn Crisps Canapes Crackers		Cheese Spread	Fish Cocktails Avocado Spread	Seed Crackers	Many	Corn Crisps Cheese Spreads	Corn Crisps Sesame Butter Canapes
Soups	Cabbage Cream	Clam Chowder Cabbage	Pea	Celery Any Type	Pea Almond	Chicken Pea Bean	Bean Borscht Tomato	Cream Garnish	Potato	Garnish	Garnish
Bread and Rolls	Coffee Cake Tea Sandwiches Bread	Rye Bread Roll Topping	Danish Pastry Buns Coffee Cake	Seed Rolls Celery Toast	Buns Bread Biscuit	Bread		Roll Topping	Sandwiches	Rolls Bread	Rolls Bread Toast Tea Sandwiches
Fish, Eggs and Cheese	Cottage Cheese	Cheddar Gorgonzola Cream Dev-illed Eggs		Fish Stews Stuffings Scrambled Eggs	Cream Cheese Cheddar	With Cheddar With Edam Deviled Eggs	Halibut Salmon Boiled Fish Cottage Cheese	Halibut Codfish Omelettes	Garnish for Fish Scalloped Fish Scalloped Eggs On any cheese		Cheese Spread
Meat and Poultry	Stews	Pork Liver Kidneys Goulash		Meat Loaf Stuffings Stews	Pork Roast Sausage Stuffing Frankfurters	Mexican Dishes Meat Loaf Chili Con Carne Chicken	Lamb Stew Creamed Chicken Chops	Liver Pork	Steaks Chops Ham Cold Cuts		Casserole Topping
Vegetables	Carrots	Turnips Sauerkraut Rice Potato Pancakes		Stewed Tomatoes	Rice Fried Potatoes Spiced Beets	Mexican Beans Sauerkraut Cabbage Rice	Sauerkraut String Beans Beets	Sauerkraut Lentils Pickled Beets	Baked Beans Green Beans Macaroni	Noodles Mashed Potatoes	Hash Browned Potatoes Noodles
Salads		Cole Slaw Beet	Orange	Aspics Fish Salads Potato	Mixed Green		Cole Slaw Potato Cucumber Avocado	Fish Mixed Green	Cole Slaw Mixed Green Salad Dressing	Pear	Potato Garnish
Cakes and Cookies	Cookies Anise Cake	Seed Cake	Danish Pastry Cookies		Cookies Gingerbread Cake Applesauce Cake	Sugar Cookies		Seed Cake Cookies		Cakes Cookies	Cookies Cakes
Desserts and Beverages	Stewed Fruits with Raw Apple Fruit Pies Tea	Baked Pears Baked Apples	Baked Apples Coffee Gelatin Demi-Tasse		Apple Pie Stewed Pears Baked Apples Rice Pudding	Fruit Pies	Apple Pie	Baked Fruit Apple Pie Pudding		Tarts	Nut Substitute
Miscellaneous	Candy	Candy	Honey Jellies Pickles	Boiled Salad Dressing Pickles	Game Sauce Pickles Candies	Cheese Toppings	Fish Sauce Olives Pickles Sour Cream	Fish Sauce Pickles Candy	Bearnaise Sauce Mayonnaise Pickles Cheese Sauce		Candy On Icings

More attractive than parsley but not as lasting. Used in a powdered combination called "Fines Herbes."

DILL—Both leaves and seeds of dill are used. Leaves may be used as a garnish or to cook with fish. Leaves or the whole plant may be used to flavor dill pickles.

MARJORAM—May be used both green and dry for flavoring soups and ragouts; and in stuffing for all meats and fish.

MINT—May be used fresh in salads, fruit beverages, jellies, conserves, ices, iced tea, sauces for meats, and added minced to carrots and peas. Good with apple combinations.

PARSLEY—One of the most popular herbs, which may be used in many ways. A favorite garnish. May be used in fruit and vegetable salads, in sandwiches, in all soups and gravies, in meat sauces, minced and added just before serving to practically all vegetables, minced and added to white sauce.

SAFFRON—Used to give pale yellow color to bread, cakes, and sauces, or to color confectionery. Has a pleasant flavor and good color.

SAGE—Used fresh and dried. May be used in poultry and meat stuffings; in sausage and practically all meat combinations; in cheese and vegetable combinations, as in vegetable loaf, or curry. The flowers are sometimes used in salads.

SAVORY—Agreeable flavor, blends well with other flavors; may be used in stuffings in meat, in vegetable soups, in sausage, with meats and with horse-radish.

SWEET BASIL—Distinct flavor of cloves. May be used for flavoring salads, soups and meats.

TARRAGON—Leaves have a hot, pungent taste. Valuable to use in all salads and sauces. Excellent in Tartar sauce. Leaves are pickled with gherkins. Used to flavor vinegar.

THYME—Leaves, green or dried, valuable for use in stuffings, sauces, soups and meats.

TYPES OF PRINCIPAL CHEESES AND WHEN TO SERVE

American Cheddar Cheese. Color ranges from pale yellow to deep orange. Young cheeses are firm and mild. Aged cheeses are sharp and crumbly. Can be used in many ways—sandwiches, snacks, toppings, crumbled, for salads and hot vegetables.

Bleu Cheese. Domestic version of Roquefort.

Brick Cheese. Light straw color and moist. Excellent for sandwiches and appetizers.

Brie Cheese. This cheese is red on the surface and the inside may vary from waxy to semi-liquid. Served mainly as an appetizer, dessert, or with salads.

Camembert Cheese. Although it has a light yellow color, it has a greyish outside rind. It is served as an appetizer or dessert or with salads.

Cheshire Cheese. This is a cheddar-type cheese. It is deep yellow in color. This cheese is usually ripened for an extended period to provide a sharp flavor.

Cottage Cheese. Also called Dutch Cheese. It is soft, white, and fluffy with a very mild flavor when not ripened. It is especially popular in salads, custards, and cheese cakes.

Cream Cheese. This is a very versatile cheese. It is mild and rich and served with crackers, used in salads, sandwiches, cheese cakes, pies, topping for fruit and other desserts. Usually one of the main ingredients for party dips.

Edam Cheese. It is red and is sold in a firm ball size. It is ripened for three weeks to three months. The flavor is similar to Cheddar and becomes sharper with longer aging. It is used in appetizers, desserts, and salads.

Emmentaler Cheese. This is the original Swiss type cheese made in Emmental, Switzerland.

English Dairy Cheese. This is also a Cheddar type cheese with a hard, sharp flavor. It grates well and is good for au gratin dishes.

Gorgonzola Cheese. Italian version of Roquefort.

Gouda Cheese. Red-coated, this cheese is golden inside. It has a slightly sweet, nut-like flavor. It is used for sandwiches, appetizers, desserts, and salads.

Gruyère Cheese. An Emmentaler type cheese, similar to Swiss. It has a nut-like flavor and a firm texture.

Hand Cheese. Very sharp. It has a pungent odor and taste.

Hvid Gjedeost. Chocolate brown in color, this is a Norwegian cheese. It is too hard to be sliced and is shaved thin and served with crackers.

Italian Cheese. There are more than twenty types of Italian cheese. The most popular are Salame, Provoloni, Provoloncinni, Provolette, Cacio Cavallo. They are cured or smoked to give a salty, tangy flavor. Mainly used to flavor soups, salads and macaroni.

Jack Cheese. In looks and taste much akin to American Cheddar Cheese.

Liederkranz Cheese. This cheese is much like Limburg Cheese.

Limburg Cheese. Of soft texture under a red-brown rind,

this cheese has a pungent flavor. It is used as a sandwich spread, in appetizers and desserts.

Muenster Cheese. This cheese is of light tan color. It has a mild flavor of caraway or anise. It is good in sandwiches, appetizers, and desserts.

Mysost Cheese. A Scandinavian cheese, it is light brown. This cheese is not ripened and has a unique sweetish taste which is very mild. It is spread on crackers and used in appetizers.

Neufchâtel Cheese. Made like cream cheese but whole or skim milk is used. This cheese is used as a base for some cheese spreads like pimiento.

Nokkelost Cheese (or Spiced Leyden). This cheese has a dark green or black exterior and is very hard. It is much like Edam but has caraway seed added. Excellent for grating and added to soups, salads, and pastas.

Pear Cheese. Also called Scarmorze, it is light tan. The cheese is usually sliced and then fried in olive oil.

Pineapple Cheese. This cheese has a bright yellow color and is hard, much like American Cheese. It is good in sandwiches, appetizers, and desserts.

Ricotta Cheese. It is pure white and has a salty taste. Excellent added to soups, salads and pastas.

Romano Cheese. This cheese is much like Parmesan and is used the same way.

Roquefort Cheese. It has a salty flavor and is crumbly when fully aged. It is a cheese for desserts, salads, and appetizers.

Sage Cheese. This cheese has a mottled green appearance. It is much like Cheddar except that green sage leaves have been added.

Sap Sago Cheese. It is a hard green cheese. It is made with clover for flavoring and is usually grated.

Swiss Cheese. This cheese is yellowish-white in color and has holes in it. It is ripened for three to six months and has a sweet or salty flavor. It is used in sandwiches, appetizers, desserts, and garnishes.

Stilton Cheese. An English cheese similar to Roquefort.

WINES
WINE CHART FOR SERVING WITH MEALS

WINE	HOW TO SERVE AND WHEN

Appetizer Wines
  Sherry
  Vermouth
	Serve chilled. Good with appetizers and soups.

Red Table Wines
  Claret
  Burgundy
	Serve cool. Excellent with spaghetti, steaks, and roasts.

White Table Wines
  Sauterne
  Rhine Wine
	Serve well-chilled. Serve with fish, chicken, and light main course dishes.

Dessert Wines
  Port
  Muscatel
	Serve cool. Good with fruits, nuts, cookies, cheeses, or sweet cakes.

Sparkling Wines
  Champagne
  Sparkling Burgundy
	Serve well chilled. Delightful with appetizers, main course, or sweets. Or for CELEBRATIONS!

Wine is a delightful companion with a meal. It makes you feel SO cosmopolitan. Enjoy this leisure when eating in your old clothes or wearing your short shorts.

soups

Soup is also impossible to prepare for one. But there are persons who could eat an entire can of soup for a meal. Served with crackers, it can make a whole meal. Or perhaps a cup of soup made from a beef bouillon cube, meat or vegetable extract, will be enough for you.

The packages of different soup flakes can come in handy too, as you can use only the desired portion and store the unused flakes in the refrigerator.

If you want to brighten up the appearance of the dish, the following garnishes are suggested:

Minced parsley
Minced chives
Minced onion tops
Slices hard cooked eggs
Fresh and dried herbs
Grated cheese, all kinds
Thin lemon slices
Radish slices
Slivers of celery rings
Sliced olives, any kind
Puffed cereal
Croutons

Perhaps tonight you want to add wine to your soups. The following chart shows what you may add to each can of soup:

Clear Soups		TABLESPOONS PORTION
Beef Bouillon	Burgundy	1 to 2
Beef Consommé		1 to 2
Beef Noodle		1 to 2
Fruit Soups (cold)		1 to 2
Thick Soups		
Baked Onion	Burgundy	1 to 2
Bean Purée		2 to 4
Oxtail		2 to 4
Pepper Pot		1 to 2
Clear Soups		
Chicken Broth	Sauterne	1 to 2
Chicken Consommé		1 to 2
Chicken Noodle		1 to 2
Cream Soups	Sauterne. Use same amount as for Sherry	
Thick Soups		
Chicken Gumbo	Sauterne	1 to 2
Oyster Gumbo		2 to 4
Tomato Bean		1 to 2
Clear Soups		
Consommé	Sherry	1 to 2
Green Turtle		2 to 4
Onion		1 to 2
Cream Soups		
Asparagus	Sherry	4 to 6
Celery		4 to 6
Mushroom		4 to 6

Thick Soups		TABLESPOONS PORTION
Black Bean	Sherry	1 to 2
Green Pea		4 to 6
Old-Fashioned		1 to 2
Purée of Bean		1 to 2
Oxtail		2 to 4
Pepper Pot		1 to 2
Scotch Broth		1 to 2
Split Pea		1 to 2

eggs

Nutritionists always say—eat at least one egg every day. It doesn't have to be a scrambled egg or a stuffed egg. Eggs are used in so many dishes that the average person usually eats one egg a day. Since eggs are found in so many of the recipes in this book, this chapter will give only a few uses for eggs.

SCRAMBLED EGG

1 large egg, well beaten
1 TBS. cream or powdered milk
Salt and pepper to taste
Cooking oil or butter to cover bottom of pan

Heat pan to 250 degrees. Blend ingredients well. Pour into pan. Start stirring immediately. When egg becomes firm, lower heat. Let stand in pan for a moment. Serve immediately.

Or: Add parsley to mixture.

Or: Add parsley and few drops of soy sauce.

OMELET

1 large egg, well beaten
2 TBS. cream or powdered milk
1 TBS. flour
  Salt and pepper to taste
  Cooking oil or butter to cover bottom of pan

Heat pan to 250 degrees. Beat all ingredients together. Pour mixture into pan. Start stirring surface immediately. When egg becomes firm, lower heat. Let stand in pan for about 5 minutes. Just before serving, fold over carefully. Remove from pan carefully.

Or: For end-of-week special, heat meat leftovers, onions, vegetables, grated cheese, or anything else you can find that is a leftover, and put in middle of omelet. Fold omelet. Serve immediately.

Or: To basic mixture sprinkle Parmesan cheese. Beat well. Follow directions as stated above.

Or: To basic mixture add ½ tsp. poppy seed. Beat well. Follow directions as stated above.

Or: To basic mixture add pinch thyme, oregano, or rosemary and parsley leaves. Follow directions above.

FRIED EGG

1 egg
  Dill seed

When egg is about half done, sprinkle with dill seed.

STUFFED HARD-COOKED EGGS

One or two stuffed hard-cooked eggs served on shredded lettuce can serve as an entire meal for the light eater. For the more hearty eater, stuffed eggs are delicious with sandwiches or a salad of your choice.

There are any number of ways to prepare stuffed hard-cooked eggs as shown below:

Slice one hard-cooked egg lengthwise, remove yolk, and fill with any of the following ingredients:

> Anchovies, minced parsley, and white sauce
> Caviar with lemon juice
> Chopped celery mixed with mayonnaise or salad dressing
> Sautéed chicken livers
> Chopped stuffed or ripe olives and cheese
> Chopped onions and mushrooms browned in butter
> Chopped nuts and cheese
> Cottage cheese, chives, pimiento, and hot sauce
> Finely ground chicken or meat
> Finely ground seasoned fish
> Liver sausage, well done
> Minced ham
> Pâté de foie gras (liver paste)
> Sardine paste

Slice one hard-cooked egg lengthwise, remove yolk. Using paring knife, cut out some of the white of the egg to use with the filler.

Combine well the removed egg yolk and filler with any of the following ingredients:

Crisp bacon, parsley, and mayonnaise
Green and red peppers, cheese
Finely chopped pickle and mayonnaise
Mayonnaise and Worcestershire sauce
Minced green peppers and mayonnaise
Minced parsley, mayonnaise, and Worcestershire sauce
Mayonnaise to moisten. Season with curry powder and
   dry mustard to taste

salads

It is a little difficult to separate the salads from the salad dressings. The guides for vegetable salads and fruit salads will make your salad making easier with its variety of ideas. Below are a few more often used recipes:

CHICKEN SALAD

  1 cup cooked or canned chicken, cut in big hunks
½ to 1 cup diced celery
    French dressing (optional)
    Mayonnaise
    Lettuce to line salad bowl or serving plate

Combine chicken, celery, mayonnaise, and French dressing. Chill for about ½ hour. Garnish with stuffed or ripe olives after arranging on lettuce leaves.

Or: Add pecans.

SALMON SALAD

  1 can salmon
  2 hard-cooked eggs, chopped

¼ cup chopped sweet pickles or pickle relish
¾ cup mayonnaise
Lettuce to line salad bowl or serving plate

Combine salmon, eggs, pickles, and mayonnaise. Arrange on lettuce leaves.

SHRIMP SALAD

1 cup cooked or canned shrimp
1 hard-cooked egg, chopped
¼ to ½ cup mayonnaise
1 tsp. lemon juice
1 TBS. minced onions
1 TBS. French dressing

Combine all ingredients. Chill. Serve on beds of shredded lettuce.

TUNA SALAD

1 7 oz. can tuna, flaked in large pieces
½ cup diced celery
½ TBS. minced onion
½ TBS. lemon juice
¼ tsp. salt
⅛ tsp. pepper
¼ tsp. dry mustard
¼ cup salad dressing or mayonnaise
Lettuce to line salad bowl or for serving plate

Combine all ingredients except lettuce. Chill. Serve on lettuce.

Or: Add 1 hard-cooked egg, finely diced.

POTATO SALAD

    2 cups potatoes, boiled, peeled, and cubed (3 medium)
    2 TBS. 1-Minute French dressing
    ¼ cup diced cucumber
    ½ cup diced celery
    ¼ onion, chopped
    1 hard-cooked egg, chopped
    6 TBS. mayonnaise
      Lettuce
      Parsley for garnish

When potatoes are prepared, pour 1-Minute French dressing over warm potatoes. Toss lightly. Cover and chill for 30 minutes. Add cucumber, celery, onion, and eggs. Then add mayonnaise and mix well with fork. Serves 3.

PORK AND BEAN SALAD

    1 can pork and beans, cold
      Diced green peppers to taste
      Onion, chopped fine, to taste
    1 heaping TBS. mayonnaise

Combine all ingredients. Serve.

CHEF SALAD

      Lettuce
    1½ tomatoes, peeled and quartered
    ½ green pepper, cut into rings
    3 radishes, sliced
    1 carrot, shredded

2 hard-cooked eggs, quartered
¼ cup French dressing
1 tsp. grated onion
1 cup meat, sliced in thin strips

Rub salad bowl with garlic. Place torn lettuce in bottom of bowl. Add vegetables and eggs. Combine dressing and onion. Add to rest of ingredients and toss. Arrange sliced meat on top. Add more dressing if desired. Makes 2 generous servings.

GUACAMOLE SALAD

1 medium avocado
⅓ tsp. chili powder
½ TBS. minced onion
Salt to taste
½ medium sized tomato
2½ TBS. French dressing

Mash avocados with onion and seasonings. Add tomato and French dressing. Mix until smooth. Serve chilled on shredded lettuce.

HERBED MACARONI SALAD

2 cups cooked macaroni
1 medium onion, finely chopped
1 small green pepper, chopped, or dehydrated green pepper, to taste
Pimiento, chopped, to taste
2½ TBS. olive or salad oil
1 TBS. vinegar
¼ tsp. salt
¼ tsp. basil

⅛ tsp. tarragon
⅛ tsp. garlic salt

Combine macaroni, onion, green pepper, and pimiento. Combine remaining ingredients and shake or stir well. Add dressing mixture to macaroni mixture and toss thoroughly.

TOMATOES STUFFED WITH SHRIMP

2 tomatoes
¼ cup cleaned shrimp, cooked or canned
2½ tsp. mayonnaise or more if desired
½ tsp. grated onion
½ tsp. minced parsley
½ tsp. minced chives or onion tops
½ tsp. chopped tarragon or tarragon vinegar

Wash tomatoes, scoop out, turn upside down to drain. Chill. Chop shrimp coarsely. Combine with remaining ingredients. Dust inside of each tomato with salt, pepper, and paprika. Fill with shrimp mixture. Extra shrimp may be served around the tomatoes.

SWISS CHEESE SALAD

1½ TBS. chopped chives or onion tops
¼ cup French dressing
½ tsp. mustard
    Salt and pepper to taste
4 oz. Swiss cheese, diced.

Combine chives, dressing and mustard. Add salt and pepper to taste. Mix with diced Swiss cheese. Let stand an hour before serving.

TONGUE SALAD

    1 cup diced cold tongue (See recipe Page 47)
    4 TBS. diced celery
    2 TBS. chopped green pepper
      Paprika to taste
      Salt and pepper to taste
    ¼ cup French dressing

Marinate tongue, celery, green pepper, and paprika. Chill
thoroughly. Serve on lettuce leaves.

CRAB MEAT SALAD

    1 cup crab meat, fresh or canned
      Paprika to taste
      Salt and pepper to taste
      French dressing, to moisten well

Mix all ingredients. Chill thoroughly. Arrange on lettuce
leaves. Spread top with mayonnaise.

LOBSTER SALAD

    1 cup cooked lobster, cut in chunks
    ¼ cup diced celery
      Salt and pepper to taste
    2 tsp. parsley leaves
    ¼ cup French dressing

Mix all ingredients. Chill thoroughly. Arrange on lettuce
leaves. Spread top with mayonnaise.

LEFTOVER MEAT SALAD

1 cup chunks of leftover meat
4 TBS. diced celery
2 TBS. chopped green pepper
2 TBS. chopped sweet, dill, or sour pickle
   Paprika to taste
   Salt and pepper to taste
¼ cup mixture of French dressing and mayonnaise
   Tarragon leaves

Combine French dressing, mayonnaise, and a few tarragon leaves. Let set for 30 minutes if possible. Chill other ingredients thoroughly before placing on lettuce leaves. Add dressing on top.

KIDNEY BEAN SALAD

4 TBS. drained kidney beans
   French dressing to moisten
2 tsp. chopped onions, onion tops, or chives
2 tsp. parsley

Moisten beans with French dressing. Sprinkle with onions, onion tops, or chives. Add parsley. Serve chilled.

ITALIAN SALAD

Torn lettuce
Diced tomatoes
Very thin slices onion
Salt and pepper to taste
Garlic powder to taste
Olive oil to moisten
Two or three flat anchovies
Few drops anchovy oil

Combine first six ingredients. Place anchovies on top of salad. Add drops of anchovy oil.

TOASTED SESAME SEED SALAD

    Lettuce, torn
½ tsp. sesame seeds, toasted light brown
1 TBS. grated Parmesan cheese
    Bleu cheese mix dressing to moisten

Combine and serve.

Or: Use Italian dressing instead of bleu cheese mix.

FRUIT SALAD GUIDE

Main Ingredient	Add. Serve on lettuce leaves.	Dressing
Red apples, sliced	Spread apple slices with cream cheese	Ginger French Dressing
Red apples, sliced	Grapefruit sections	Ambrosia French Dressing
Apple wedges, cooked in cinnamon candy syrup	Avocado, pared and sliced	1-Minute French Dressing
Diced apples	Halved raw cranberries Diced celery	Creamy French Dressing
Diced apples	Diced celery Orange sections	Wesson Mayonnaise
Diced apples	Chopped celery Nuts Seeded Tokay grapes	1-Minute French Dressing
Crushed pineapple	Chopped cucumber Lettuce	Wesson Mayonnaise
Pineapple chunks (fresh or canned)	Sliced bananas Diced celery	Cooked Mayonnaise

FRUIT SALAD GUIDE (*Continued*)
Add. Serve on lettuce leaves.

Main Ingredient		Dressing
Pineapple chunks (fresh or canned)	Melon balls	Mint French Dressing
Sliced pineapple (fresh or canned)	Cream cheese Chopped nuts	1-Minute French Dressing
Sliced pineapple (fresh or canned)	Grapefruit sections Orange sections	Nectar Dressing
Sliced pineapple (fresh or canned)	Prunes, stuffed with cream cheese	1-Minute French Dressing
Sliced pineapple (fresh or canned)	Peach halves Cottage cheese	Creamy French Dressing
Bananas, sliced	Red apples, sliced	Nectar Dressing
Bananas, sliced	Shredded cabbage	Wesson Mayonnaise with prepared mustard added
Bananas, sliced	Grapefruit sections and orange sections	Honey French Dressing

VEGETABLE SALAD GUIDE

Main Ingredient	Add	Dressing
Shredded cabbage	Chopped onion Thinly sliced carrots	Olive French Dressing
Shredded cabbage	Chopped green pepper Chopped pimiento	Garlic French Dressing Dash Tabasco
Shredded cabbage	Drained pineapple chunks	Fluffy Cream Dressing with extra salt, to taste
Shredded cabbage	Salted peanuts	1-Minute French Dressing
Shredded cabbage	Chopped celery Chopped parsley	Thousand Island French Dressing
Shredded cabbage	Unpared red apples, diced	Cooked Mayonnaise with extra salt, to taste

VEGETABLE SALAD GUIDE (*Continued*)

Main Ingredient	Add	Dressing
Shredded cabbage	Minced green pepper Minced onion	Celery Seed French Dressing
Tomatoes, cut into eighths	Chopped onion Capers	Celery Seed French Dressing
Tomatoes, sliced	Sliced cucumber	Garlic French Dressing
Tomatoes, cut in very thin vertical slices	Minced parsley Minced green onions Freshly ground black pepper	1-Minute French Dressing
Tomatoes, cut into eighths	Head lettuce, broken into bite-size pieces	Onion French Dressing
Tomatoes, sliced	Avocado, pared and cut into strips	1-Minute French Dressing
Tomatoes, sliced	Cottage cheese	Chive French Dressing
Tomatoes, centers removed	Diced cooked chicken	Creamy French Dressing
Cucumber, sliced	Green or sweet onions, sliced	1-Minute French Dressing
Cucumber, sliced	Sliced tomatoes	Garlic French Dressing
Cucumber, sliced	Sliced radishes Green pepper strips	Onion French Dressing
Cucumber, chopped	Chopped onion Hearts of lettuce	Creamy French Dressing
Cucumber, with center removed	Fill cucumber with seasoned cream cheese. Slice and arrange on lettuce	1-Minute French Dressing
Cucumber, sliced	Sliced onions Lettuce chunks Tomato wedges	1-Minute French Dressing

salad dressings

If you like salads, you can have a lot of fun experimenting with dressings. Here are a number of dressings that are not only pleasing to look at heaped on your favorite salad, but easy to prepare, as well as tasty. If these aren't enough to tempt you, the grocery shelves are filled with all types—for the calorie conscious—the "diet-watcher"—and lucky you who can eat anything.

SALAD DRESSING MIXES

You can find many excellent salad dressing mixes at your favorite grocer's. In place of water, you can use the following:

White wine	Tomato juice
Red wine	Sour cream
Vermouth	Mayonnaise
Chili sauce	Fruit juices
Catsup	Canned tomato soup
V-8 juice	Red wine and 2 TBS. grated Parmesan cheese

Or: You can use ¼ cup of any of these liquids in addition to water.

NEW ORLEANS DRESSING

- 1 tsp. salt
- ½ tsp. sugar
- ¼ tsp. pepper
- ½ tsp. paprika
- ½ tsp. dry mustard
- ¾ cup Wesson oil
- ¾ cup vinegar (or cider, malt, tarragon or wine vinegar, or lemon juice)
- ½ tsp. Worcestershire sauce

Measure into jar in order given. Cover. Shake.

Or: Add ¼ cup Roquefort-type cheese.

Or: Add chopped hard-cooked egg.

Or: 1 TBS. chopped onion

WESSON 1-MINUTE FRENCH DRESSING

- 2 tsp. salt
- 1 tsp. sugar
- ½ tsp. pepper
- 1 tsp. paprika
- ½ cup vinegar (or cider, malt, tarragon or wine vinegar, or lemon juice)
- 1½ cups Wesson oil

Combine and shake well in covered jar. Shake well before using. Makes 2 cups.

VARIETIES OF WESSON 1-MINUTE FRENCH DRESSING

Name of Dressing	Start with Wesson 1-Minute French Dressing	Add	Good with these Salads
Ambrosia	½ cup	¼ cup sugar ¼ tsp. celery seed 1 TBS. catsup	Fruit
Anchovy	½ cup	½ TBS. chopped parsley 1 TBS. anchovy paste ½ TBS. chopped onion	Mixed Greens Egg Salad
Bleu Cheese	½ cup	2 TBS. crumbled Bleu Cheese	Head Lettuce Orange and Onion Grapefruit Tomatoes and Greens Vegetable
Celery Seed	½ cup	1 TBS. catsup 2 tsp. sugar ¼ tsp. celery seed 1 clove peeled garlic	
Chiffonade	1 cup	1 hard-cooked egg, chopped 1 small beet, finely chopped 1 small onion, finely chopped	Hearts of Lettuce
Chili	½ cup	½ tsp. sugar 2 TBS. chili sauce	Meat Fish Vegetable
Chive	½ cup	1 to 2 TBS. finely cut chives	Mixed Greens Tuna Potato
Creamy	½ cup with lemon juice	1/3 cup light cream. Add gradually. Beat with rotary beater until thick	Fruit Chicken Potato
Creole	½ cup with lemon juice	¼ cup catsup ½ tsp. Worcestershire sauce Dash Tabasco	Vegetable Meat Fish
Curry	½ cup	⅛ tsp. curry powder	Greens Fish Meat

VARIETIES OF WESSON 1-MINUTE FRENCH DRESSING (*Cont.*)

Name of Dressing	Start with Wesson 1-Minute French Dressing	Add	Good with these Salads
Garlic	½ cup	1 clove peeled garlic. Remove before serving	Any Green Salad Some Fruit Salads
Ginger	½ cup	1 TBS. chopped crystallized ginger	Fruit
Herb	½ cup	2 tsp. chopped parsley ⅛ tsp. powdered thyme ½ tsp. powdered oregano Salt as desired	Greens
Honey	½ cup	2 tsp. lemon juice 2 tsp. honey ¾ tsp. sugar ¼ tsp. grated lemon rind	Fruit
Indienne	½ cup	¼ tsp. curry powder 1 TBS. India relish	Greens Fish Egg
Ketchup, Catchup, or Catsup	½ cup	¼ cup ketchup, catchup, or catsup	Greens Meat
Lorenzo	½ cup	½ cup chili sauce ½ cup chopped water cress 1 tsp. onion juice	Shrimp Lobster Crab
Mint	½ cup with lemon juice	2 TBS. finely chopped mint	Fruit
Mixed Garden	½ cup	1 tsp. celery seed 2 tsp. finely chopped onion 2 TBS. finely chopped green pepper	Vegetable
Olive	½ cup	2 TBS. finely chopped ripe or stuffed olives	Vegetable
Onion	½ cup	1 TBS. chopped onion Dash of Tabasco	Greens Grapefruit Orange

VARIETIES OF WESSON 1-MINUTE FRENCH DRESSING (*Cont.*)

Name of Dressing	Start with Wesson 1-Minute French Dressing	Add	Good with these Salads
Vinaigrette	½ cup	2 hard-cooked egg yolks, mashed 2 TBS. chopped green pepper 1 TBS. chopped onion	Vegetable

HERB MARINADE DRESSING

For each salad:
    Salt and pepper to taste
   3 tsp. sweet pickle juice
   1 tsp. salad oil
    Lemon juice to taste
    Garlic salt
  ¼ tsp. marjoram
  ¼ tsp. thyme

Scatter above ingredients in order or mixed up. It doesn't make any difference. Cover the salad. In about an hour toss salad with fork. The longer this dressing blends with the salad, made up of lettuce, tomatoes, etc., the tastier it will get.

ROQUEFORT-RUM SALAD DRESSING

To French dressing, add ½ cup Roquefort cheese blended with ¼ cup rum. Serve on Chef's Salad Bowl.

WESSON OIL MAYONNAISE

  1 egg or 2 egg yolks
  3 TBS. lemon juice or vinegar

1 tsp. salt
1 tsp. sugar
1 tsp. dry mustard
½ tsp. paprika
2 cups Wesson oil

Beat egg with one TBS. of lemon juice, using rotary beater or electric mixer. Add salt, sugar, dry mustard, and paprika, beating until well blended. Add Wesson oil, little at a time, beating constantly, until a thick mixture forms. As mayonnaise thickens, oil can be added more rapidly, beating constantly. When dressing is very thick, beat in remaining lemon juice or vinegar. Then add remaining oil gradually, beating until well blended. Makes 2¼ cups.

RUSSIAN DRESSING

½ cup mayonnaise
¼ cup chili sauce
¼ cup chopped sweet gherkins
¼ tsp. celery seed

Combine all ingredients. Mix well. Excellent on Open Face Sandwich (See Page 149)

WESSON COOKED DRESSING (MAYONNAISE)

⅓ cup flour
1 tsp. sugar
1 tsp. salt
1 tsp. dry mustard
¾ cup water
¼ cup vinegar or lemon juice
2 eggs or 4 egg yolks
1 cup Wesson oil

Mix dry ingredients in heavy 1-quart saucepan. Add water and vinegar gradually, stirring until smooth. Cook over low heat, stirring until mixture boils. Boil 1 minute. Remove from heat. Pour into bowl. With rotary beater, beat in eggs. Continue beating, adding oil gradually. Chill. Makes about 2 cups.

THOUSAND ISLAND DRESSING

- 1 cup mayonnaise
- 1/4 cup chopped celery
- 1/4 cup chopped ripe olives
- 2 TBS. chopped green pepper
- 1 hard-cooked egg, finely chopped
- 1/2 cup chili sauce
- 2 tsp. grated onion
- 1 tsp. salt

Mix all ingredients. Serve on head lettuce or other green, or cooked vegetables, meat or fish salads. Makes 2 cups. Can store in refrigerator for some time.

meats

Like finding fresh vegetables in season, you will find that fresh meats found in markets are regional. People in different parts of the country prefer different cuts and types of meat. Even in a large town you will find meat markets will vary as to cuts and kinds of meat available, according to their trade.

You don't need a course in the art of buying meat to find the proper cuts. The best advice is to know your butcher and to know him well. If he is interested in building his trade, he will be helpful in selecting the size of cuts you want and give you valuable cooking hints, which will help you to easily prepare the following recipes.

AMOUNTS OF MEATS, POULTRY, AND FISH TO BUY

The following guide for two is only suggestive. There are some foods that do not cook well unless they are in ample portions. So, in order to eat some of these items, you will have to buy enough for two or more, cook, fry, boil, or whatever, and freeze the balance.

	For 2

BEEF

Corned Beef	1 lb. piece
Dried Beef (for creaming)	⅛ lb.
Hamburgers—ground chuck, round, rump	¾ lb.
Oxtails (braised)	1
Pot Roast—boned chuck, round, or rump	3 lb. piece (about 3 meals)
Rib Roast, Standing	1 rib (about 3 meals)
Short Ribs (to braise with vegetables)	1 lb.
Steak:	
Club	1 steak, 1½″ thick
Cube	2 steaks, ½″ thick
Filet Mignon	2 steaks, 1″ to 1½″ thick
Rib	1 steak, 2″ thick
Sirloin	1 steak, 1″ thick
Swiss (to braise), boned chuck, round, or rump	1 lb. steak, 1″ thick
Stew Meat—boned chuck, round, or rump	1 lb.
Tongue	1, smallest size

LAMB

Breast, boned	2 lbs.
Chops:	
English	2, 1½″ to 2″ thick
Loin or Rib, 1-Rib	4, ¾″ thick
Loin or Rib, double rib	2, 1½″ thick
Shoulder	2, ¾″ to 1″ thick
Heart (braised)	1 or 2
Kidneys	2
Liver	¾ lb.

	For 2

LAMB

Patties—ground breast, flank, neck, or
  shoulder .... ¾ lb.

Roasts:

    Crown Roast .... 3 lbs.
         (2 or more meals)

    Sirloin End of Leg .... 2 to 3 lbs.
         (2 or more meals)

Shanks (braised) 2

Steaks (from leg-pan broil) .... 2, ½″ to 1″ thick

Stew Meat—boned, neck, breast, or
  shoulder .... 1 lb.

Tongue .... 4 ea.

PORK—FRESH

Chops (always braised)

    Loin .... 2, ¾″ to 1¼″ thick
    Rib .... 2, ¾″ to 1¼″ thick

Roasts:

    Loin .... 3 to 4 lbs.
         (2 or more meals)

    Rolled Shoulder .... 3 to 4 lbs.
         (2 or more meals)

Shoulder Steaks 2

Spareribs .... 1 side, 1½ to 2 lbs.

Tenderloin 1

PORK—SMOKED

Ham

    Butt End .... About 5 lbs.
         (several meals)

    Picnic Shoulder .... About 5 lbs.
         (several meals)

    Slice (cooked or uncooked) .... 1 slice, ½″ to 1″ thick

    Boneless, Smoked Shoulder Butt 1½ to 2 lbs.
         (several meals)

	For 2

PORK—SMOKED

Bacon:
    Canadian Bacon .... ½ lb. sliced, ¼″ thick
    Sliced Bacon .... ½ lb., 8 to 10 slices
Pork Sausage:
    Bulk—Country Style or Smoked . ½ lb.
    Cellophane Rolls .... ½ or 1 lb. roll
    Links .... ½ lb.
    Patties .... ½ lb.

SAUSAGES—READY TO EAT MEATS:

Frankfurters 2
Bologna .... ¼ to ½ lb.
Jellied Tongue .... ¼ to ½ lb.
Liver Loaf (or Liver Cheese) .... ⅜ lb.
Liver Sausage .... ¼ to ⅜ lb.
Luncheon Meat .... ¼ to ⅜ lb.
Meat Loaf .... ¼ to ⅜ lb.
Salami (cooked) .... ⅙ to ¼ lb.
Salami (hard) .... ⅙ to ¼ lb.
Thuringer Summer Sausage .... ⅙ to ¼ lb.

VEAL

Calf Brains 2
Calf Heart .... 1 or 2
Calf Liver .... ½ to ¾ lb., ½″ to ¾″
                                thick
Calf Sweetbreads .... 1 pair
Chops (braised)
    Loin or Rib .... 2, ¾″ to 1″ thick
Cutlets (braised) .... 1 lb.
Kidneys .... 2, split

For 2

VEAL

Roasts:
    Loin .... 2½ to 3 lbs.
                            (several meals)
    Boned Rump or Round .... 3 lbs. (several meals)
    Rolled Shoulder .... 3–4 lbs.
                            (several meals)

Steaks:
    Round (braised) .... ¾ to 1 lb.
    Shoulder .... ¾ to 1 lb.
Stew Meat—boned shank, shoulder,
rump, neck .... 1 lb.

POULTRY

Broiler .... 1 whole
Duck .... 3½ to 4 lbs. drawn
                            (about 3 meals)
Fryer .... 1¾ to 2 lbs., drawn
                            1½ to 2 lbs., drawn
Turkey .... Half turkey
                            (several meals)

FISH

Fillets .... ¾ lb.
Steaks .... 1 lb.
Whole .... 1½ lb.

MEATS

Although you will not find recipes for all the entrées shown
in the wine chart below, you will find the wines needed if
you use other recipes.

Entrées	Type of Wine	Cup portions
Beef Stew	Burgundy	¼ cup, just before serving
Goulash	Burgundy	⅛ to ¼ cup, just before serving
Hamburgers	Burgundy	⅛ to ¼ cup, just before serving
Luncheon Meats	Burgundy	¼ cup, basted during cooking
Pot Roast	Burgundy	½ cup. Add wine last half of cooking period
Lamb Roast	Sauterne	¼ cup last half of cooking period
Veal Roast	Sauterne	½ cup. Baste with wine during roasting
Spaghetti Dinner (Meatless)	Burgundy	2 to 4 TBS., just before serving
Spaghetti (With meat sauce)	Burgundy	2 to 4 TBS., just before serving

BEEF (ROASTS)

Since roasts lose their flavor in smaller amounts than three lbs., it is suggested that you order roast beef on those special occasions when you eat out.

BRAISED SHORT RIBS OF BEEF WITH VEGETABLES

½ lb. short ribs of beef
½ TBS. flour
½ tsp. salt
⅛ tsp. pepper
1 tsp. fat

½ cup boiling water
1 halved med. potato
2 small onions
2 quartered carrots

Dredge meat with flour, salt, and pepper. Brown well on all sides in fat in small deep skillet. Or brown in frying pan and then put meat in sauce pan. Add water, cover, simmer over low heat 2 hours. Add vegetables and cook, covered, 20 minutes or until both meat and vegetables are tender.

HUNGARIAN GOULASH

¾ TBS. cooking oil
¾ cup thinly sliced onions
1½ tsp. salt
¼ tsp. paprika
6 to 8 oz. chuck, rump, or rounded beef, in 1″ cubes, or ground beef in chunks
1 tsp. paprika
¾ cup water
½ bay leaf
Caraway seed

Sauté onions and salt in cooking oil. Add ¼ tsp. paprika and meat. Mix well. Cover. Simmer over very low heat 1 hour. Add 1 tsp. paprika and water to just cover meat. Put contents in sauce pan. Add bay leaf. Cover. Cook 1 hour or until tender. Shortly before goulash is ready, add caraway seed. Add more water towards end of cooking.

Or: Can be served on noodles.

Or: Add 1 small potato, diced, last hour of simmering.

BEEF ROLLS

½ lb. round beef, ¼" thick
1 small dill pickle
1 slice bacon
1 small peeled onion, thinly sliced
  Salt and pepper to taste
  Salad oil for frying skillet

Cut beef in two strips. Cut pickle in two. Cut bacon in half. On each strip of beef, place crosswise pickle, bacon, and 2 onion slices. Sprinkle with salt and pepper, tie with string. Sauté in fat in skillet until brown. Remove to heavy sauce pan, barely cover with hot water, let simmer covered, 2 hours or until tender. Add more water if needed.

BARBECUED BEEF (OR ANY TYPE MEAT)

8 oz. meat, any type, sliced, ¼" to ½" thick, 1" wide
  Tenderizer
  Barbecue sauce

Use tenderizer on meat and let set at least one hour. Heat oven to 350 degrees. Brown meat. Remove meat to flat pan. Baste with barbecue sauce about every 15 minutes until meat is tender.

Or: If you want to use an electric skillet, brown meat in it and then remove meat from skillet. Clean skillet. Using aluminum wrap, fashion a small sauce pan with sides turned up enough so that liquid will not ooze out. Baste with barbecue sauce about every 15 minutes. Set skillet at 250 degrees for first 30 minutes. Last 30 minutes set skillet at 200 degrees

ALUMINUM WRAP STEAK

Individual serving of steak
Small potato cut in ½″ slices
Sliced onion
Two carrots sliced down middle

Place all ingredients on heavy aluminum wrap, with onions on top. Seal wrap around ingredients. Place in shallow pan. Bake in very hot oven for 30 minutes or until done.

Or: If chuck steak is used, be sure to use tenderizer. Put in potato and carrots whole. Bake about 1 hour or until done.

INDIVIDUAL CHUCK ROAST STEAKS

Buy 3 to 4 lb. chuck roast, with as little bone as possible. If you are lucky your market manager will cut this meat up into serving pieces for you—about 8 oz. in each serving. Using toothpicks, make flat pieces into fillet shape. Pieces of meat left over can be used for stew, chili, or soup.

Wrap each piece in freezing paper and freeze. Remove from freezing unit as needed.

Individual serving of meat
Tenderizer
Salt and pepper to taste
Garlic powder, if desired

Tenderize steak for at least 1 hour before cooking. Just before putting in heavy skillet add seasoning—or later if desired. Fry first at about 300 degrees until brown on bottom and blood comes to surface on top. Turn. Lower heat until about 225 degrees. Remove from heat when meat is still slightly pink inside. Remember, meat cooks for a moment or two after leaving pan.

Or: For added seasoning, put thick slices of onion on top of steak while frying.

Or: Wrap bacon around meat and cook.

GROUND MEAT DISHES

Many people who live and eat alone buy ground meat. It can easily be bought in small amounts, and there are many ways to prepare it. In these recipes, I recommend beef over other types of meat.

FILLED PATTIE BURGERS

½ lb. ground beef
   Salt and pepper to taste
   Garlic to taste
 2 tsp. dried parsley
 2 to 3 slices onion
 6 1″ strips American cheese

Season beef to taste. Add parsley. Divide meat in half. Make two or three patties, very thin, with one half. Place slice onion on these halves. Cover with balance of meat, flattened out thin. Mash edges together. Broil in oven. When almost done, place two strips cheese on each burger. Sprinkle cheese with parsley. Heat until cheese is melted. Burgers can also be pan fried on top of stove. After adding cheese and parsley, cover pan, and steam until cheese has melted.

Or: Instead of filling with onion, use mixture of 2 TBS. bleu cheese, 1 TBS. mayonnaise, ½ TBS. Worcestershire sauce, ¼ tsp. dry mustard.

Or: Instead of filling with onion, use mixture of 1 TBS. melted butter, ¾ cup fine fresh bread crumbs, ¼ tsp. dried thyme, little minced onion, ½ tsp. lemon juice.

Or: Fill with 1 slice tomato, thick, and 1 slice cheese. Follow directions above.

Or: Wrap bacon around each pattie and fry.

PLAIN BURGERS

½ lb. ground beef
Salt and pepper to taste
Garlic if preferred

Makes three patties. Fry in cooking oil until done. Can also be broiled.

Or: Add ¾ cup bread crumbs and make five or six patties.

Or: Spread mixture on saltines, completely covering each. Broil 2 min. or until brown. Serve immediately as saltines will get soft.

Or: Spread on bread which has been toasted on one side. Bake in oven or broiler.

Or: After patties are partially done, spread plain mustard or horse-radish mustard on one side. Continue cooking until done.

Or: Make mixture of butter, chopped onion, and Angostura bitters to taste. Spread on one side of burgers when almost done. Continue cooking until done.

Or: When burgers are almost done, sprinkle any type of cheese or cheese spread on one side of burgers. Continue cooking until done.

Or: With ½ lb. ground beef add ½ pkg. onion soup mix.
NO OTHER SEASONING IS NEEDED.

HAWAIIAN HAMBURGERS

½ lb. ground beef
½ onion, finely chopped
½ clove garlic, very finely chopped
¼ cup soy sauce
⅛ tsp. ground ginger

Mix beef and onion. Shape into four patties, ½ inch thick.
Combine garlic, soy sauce, and ginger. Pour over patties. Let
stand at least 30 minutes. Remove patties from sauce. Broil
on pan about 3 inches from heat source, 5 to 7 minutes on
each side. Or, can be pan fried in 2 TBS. hot fat.

MEAT LOAF

½ lb. ground beef
  Salt to taste
  Pepper to taste
  Garlic to taste
½ chopped onion
 1 slice soft white bread, crumbed
 1 beaten egg
½ cup tomato juice, or ½ cup boullion (make with 1
  cube)
¼ tsp. dry mustard

Combine all ingredients. Place loaf on heavy aluminum wrap,
shaped like a pan, but leave open. Bake in 425 degree oven
for about 30 minutes.

Or: About 15 minutes before loaf is done, you can pour catsup on top for color.

Or: If using electric skillet bake in oiled pan at 185 for about 45 minutes. Turn once to brown top.

Or: Instead of white bread, use rye bread.

INDIVIDUAL MEAT AND NOODLE DISH

½ lb. ground meat, pressed in bite-size chunks
   Salt and pepper to taste
1 onion, diced
2 boullion cubes diluted in one cup water
¼ cup uncooked noodles
¼ cup cooking wine

Brown meat and onions. Add diluted boullion. Simmer until meat is tender in deep sauce pan for about 30 minutes. Add *uncooked* noodles. Boil slowly for fifteen minutes. Add wine. Simmer slowly for five more minutes. If you want to thicken liquid, gradually add 2 tsp. flour.

Or: Instead of using raw onion, at last add herbed onions (See page 95).

ITALIAN SPAGHETTI

½ lb. ground meat, beef preferred
½ small onion, chopped fine
½ slice bread, crumbed fine
1 egg (optional)
   Parsley
   Parmesan cheese
   Salt to taste
   Ground pepper to taste
   Olive oil

Combine all of above, except olive oil, lightly. Form into 1 inch balls. Brown in hot olive oil.

Sauce:

> 1 onion, small, diced
> 1 garlic button, diced
> 1 8 oz. can tomato sauce
> 1 cup water
> ¾ tsp. Italian spaghetti seasoning
> Olive oil

Sauté onions and garlic in olive oil. Add tomato sauce, water, and spaghetti seasoning. Bring to boil. Add meat balls. Cover. Simmer for 1 hour or until sauce is a dark red. Serve on spaghetti (See page 71).

CORNED BEEF

Since corned beef tastes better cold and freezes so well, you will probably want to use this recipe sometime. Cut up and freeze in meal size portions.

> 2 to 3½ lb. corned beef brisket
> 4 garlic buds slivered
> 8 whole cloves
> 2 bay leaves
> 1 tsp. ground pepper
> 2 sliced onions

Soak the meat in cold water for 15 minutes. Drain and stick with cloves and slivers of garlic buds. Put meat in large kettle. Add bay leaves, ground pepper, and onions. Cover with water and simmer very slowly for 3 to 3½ hours, or until easily pierced with fork.

FRANKFURTERS

Frankfurters are completely cooked when bought. They only need to be heated to serve hot.

Boiled. Put frankfurters in boiling water to cover. Remove pan from heat, cover, and let stand 7 to 8 minutes.

Sautéed. Sauté frankfurters in fat or salad oil for 5 to 6 minutes, turning once.

Broiled. For *whole* frankfurter, brush with melted butter, or wrap in bacon strips, secured with toothpicks.

For *split* frankfurter, fill with relish, mashed potato, cooked rice, cheese, or mustard. Brush with melted butter, or wrap with bacon strips, secured with toothpicks.

Broil whole or split frankfurters for 5 to 6 min. Turn often. Leftover frankfurters: Slice or cut up and add to vegetable salads or soups.

BARBECUED FRANKFURTERS

  1 TBS. salad oil
2½ TBS. minced onion
  ⅜ tsp. paprika
  ⅛ tsp. pepper
  1 tsp. granulated sugar
  ⅜ tsp. dry mustard
1½ tsp. Worcestershire sauce
1½ TBS. catsup
  1 TBS. vinegar
  2 frankfurters

Melt fat, add onion, and simmer until tender. Add next 7 ingredients. Slit each frankfurter 3″ through center. Arrange in baking pan, slit side up, and pour sauce over all. Bake in moderate oven of 350 degrees, 20 minutes, basting several times.

WEENIES HORS D'OEUVRES

(SEE SNACKS & DIPS, PAGE 162)

LAMB

Lamb roasts, as with other kinds of meat, lose their best flavor in less than 3 lb. sizes. When eating out, and lamb roast is your favorite dish, it is suggested that you order it then.

LAMB CHOPS

Lamb chops are usually cut in four different types: Rib Lamb Chops, Loin Lamb Chops, English Lamb Chops, and Shoulder Lamb Chops.

> 2 Rib or Loin Lamb Chops or 1 English or Shoulder Lamb Chop.

Preheat broiler for 10 minutes. Snip outer edge of fat at 1″ intervals. Sprinkle with salt and pepper. Rub broiler rack with fat from meat. Arrange chops on greased rack from 1½″ to 2″ below heat. Broil 10 to 20 minutes on each side, according to thickness of chops. Check desired doneness by making a cut in flesh along bone.

PORK

Pork roasts, as with other kinds of meat, lose their best flavor in small portions. It is suggested that you order pork roast at your favorite restaurant.

PORK CHOPS

2 small pork chops

Trim off extra fat. Cut outer edges on slat at 1″ intervals. Sprinkle lightly with salt and pepper. Add garlic if desired. Place chops in hot skillet, brown well on both sides, about 15 to 20 minutes. Remove excess fat as it accumulates. Add ⅓ to ½ cup boiling water, canned tomatoes, tomato sauce, cream, or tomato juice, canned pineapple syrup, or barbecue sauce. Simmer in covered pan for about 1 hour or until chops can be cut very easily. Add more seasoning if desired.

FRESH PORK SAUSAGE

Pork sausage must be cooked well done. It should not be dry and crisp. Fry over low heat 12 to 15 minutes until no pink remains, turning often.

To bake, arrange sausage links or patties in baking pan. Bake for ½ hour in hot oven, until no pink remains.

HAM

Baking a ham for one person's use is fine if you want to make one meal and sandwiches that will last you for a week.

BAKED HAM

1 ham, small as possible
Cloves
Mustard

Place ham, fat side up, in uncovered roasting pan. Slash rind in diamond shape. At intersections, insert cloves. About half way during baking, put mustard on ham for added flavoring.

Some cooks prefer to wrap ham in aluminum foil and bake. If ham is wrapped in foil, put mustard on ham before putting in oven.

Bake in 325 degree oven, about 25 minutes for each pound.

GLAZED CANNED BAKED HAM

Canned hams can be bought in as small as 3 lb. sizes.

Heat ham, allowing 15 to 20 minutes per pound in 325 degree oven. About 20 minutes before being thoroughly heated, spread with one of the following:

6 TBS. canned crushed pineapple and 6 TBS. brown sugar.

Or: ½ cup brown sugar mixed with juice and grated rind 1 orange.

Or: ½ cup brown or white sugar, mixed with ½ tsp. powdered mustard and 1 or 2 TBS. vinegar, fruit juice or cider, or ½ tsp. bottled horse-radish.

Or: Pat mustard on ham, dot with cloves a few inches apart.

HAM SLICES

Ham slices can be bought in desired amount. Slice off enough for one serving. Freeze balance.

Pan fry over medium heat, 6 to 8 minutes.

LIVER

Calves liver is more popular than beef, lamb, or pork liver.

PAN FRIED LIVER

¼ to ½ lb. liver
Flour for patting
Salt and pepper to taste

Wipe liver clean. Snip out tubes in liver with scissors. Pat flour in liver—not heavily—salt and pepper. Sauté quickly in hot greased skillet until brown on one side, turn, brown on other side.

LIVER PATTIES

¼ to ½ lb. liver
½ onion cut up
½ tsp. salt
Speck pepper
Fat or salad oil to coat bottom of skillet.

Put liver and onion through food chopper. Use medium blade. Combine salt and pepper. Heat fat in skillet. Make about five patties, 3″ in diameter. Sauté over medium heat until brown on both sides and cooked thoroughly.

TONGUE

Tongue is usually inexpensive. You can buy calf, beef, lamb, or pork tongues. Calf and beef are more desirable. Leftover for serving for one can be frozen or used for sandwiches.

BOILED TONGUE

   1 small tongue
   1 bay leaf
   2 or 3 whole cloves
   1 sliced large onion
   1 tsp. peppercorns
   2 peeled cloves garlic
1½ tsp. salt

Put tongue in deep kettle. Cover completely with warm water. Bring to boil. Add balance of ingredients. Cover. Simmer about 50 minutes per pound, or until a fork pierces easily. Let tongue cool 1 hr. in liquor. Remove. Pull off skin carefully. Serve hot or cold with mustard, horse-radish, or any bottled sauce.

TONGUE SALAD (SEE PAGE 47)

VEAL

Veal roasts, as with other kinds of meat, lose their best flavor in less than 3 lb. sizes. It is suggested that you make it easy on yourself and order veal roast when eating out.

BRAISED VEAL CHOPS

   Flour mixed with salt and pepper to taste
   1 loin or rib veal chop, ¾″ thick
¼ TBS. salad oil
¼ cup water, tomato juice, or sauterne wine
¼ TBS. flour
¾ TBS. cold water
   Salt and pepper

Place seasoned flour in shallow plate. Coat chop on both sides. Heat fat in skillet. Sauté chops until well browned on both sides. Add liquid. Cover and simmer about 45 minutes or until chop is tender. Just before removing chop from skillet, blend 1/4 TBS. flour with 3/4 TBS. water to smooth paste. Add little hot liquid from skillet. Remove chop. Stir paste into liquid in skillet. Add salt and pepper. Heat until smooth and thick, then pour over chop.

BREADED VEAL CUTLETS

   1/4 lb. veal cutlet, 1/2" thick
     1 small egg
 1 1/2 TBS. milk
   1/4 TBS. salad oil
      Salt and pepper to taste
 1 1/2 TBS. flour
      Finely sifted dried bread crumbs
 1 1/2 TBS. salad oil

Flatten veal to 1/4" thickness, or ask butcher to flatten meat for you. Cut into serving pieces. Beat egg slighly with fork, stir in milk, salad oil, salt, and pepper. Put flour and bread crumbs in separate flat dishes. Roll veal in flour and then in beaten egg and then in bread crumbs. Heat fat in skillet over low heat, sauté slowly until well-browned on both sides and very tender. Allow about 15 minutes for each side.

VENISON STEAKS

   2 venison steaks
    Tenderizer
    Salt and pepper to taste
    Garlic, optional
    Olive oil and cooking oil combined for frying

Sprinkle steaks with tenderizer and rub in olive oil and garlic, salt, and pepper, 1 hour before frying. Fry slowly in a combination of cooking oil and olive oil until well done.

chicken

One nice thing about chicken these days is that you don't have to buy it "on foot." You can buy it frozen, whole, or all legs, or all breasts, or whatever you wish. Or you can buy a half chicken in the market, dressed and cut up to suit your needs. Or you can buy a whole chicken, use what you need, and freeze the balance until you are "chicken-minded" again.

If you prepare more chicken than you need for one serving, you won't mind the leftovers. Sometimes they taste much better cold.

BAKED CHICKEN DINNER

½ frozen chicken fryer, partly thawed
2½ TBS. French or Italian salad dressing
    Salt, pepper, and paprika to taste
    Chopped parsley

Thaw chicken until pieces can be separated. Heat oven to 375 degrees. Brush chicken with ⅓ of salad dressing. Sprinkle with salt, pepper and paprika. Place chicken in shallow baking dish. Bake uncovered 50 to 55 minutes, or until golden brown and tender. Turn chicken two or three times and brush with remaining dressing while baking. Sprinkle with chopped parsley before serving, if desired.

CHICKEN IN CREAM

½ of three pound chicken, or whatever amount desired
4 TBS. fat
1 TBS. minced onion
1 cup thin cream
¼ to ½ tsp. thyme

Cut chicken as for frying. Dip in milk, roll in flour to which salt has been added. Fry in hot fat until nicely browned. Place in small shallow baking dish, add onion. Pour cream over chicken. Do not cover. Put back in oven. Heat until cream is bubbly.

FRIED CHICKEN

Fryer, cut in frying pieces. Use enough for one serving.
Flour
Pepper
Salt
Cooking oil, to cover chicken half way in skillet

Salt chicken well about one hour before frying. Dry well with paper towels. Mix flour and pepper in small sack. Using about two pieces at a time, shake chicken well in sack. Fry, about 275 degrees heat, skin down with pan covered. Fry until golden brown. Remove cover, turn over pieces, turn up heat until about 325 degrees. Fry until chicken is browned to desired doneness.

Or: Add parsley leaves and Parmesan cheese to flour mixture.

Or: Instead of salting chicken for one hour, marinate chicken in soy sauce. Dry well before shaking in flour and pepper mixture.

Or: Add tarragon leaves to flour mixture.

Or: Add ½ tsp. paprika and ¼ tsp. powdered mustard to 4 TBS. flour. Follow directions above.

BAKED-FRIED CHICKEN

> ½ fryer, or number of pieces of chicken desired
> Flour to coat chicken
> ¾ cup water
> 1 TBS. Worcestershire sauce
> ½ bay leaf
> 1 TBS. sherry or other wine
> Garlic

Salt chicken 24 hours ahead of time if possible. Dry with paper towels. Roll in flour or put flour in sack and coat chicken that way. Cover bottom of frying skillet with salad oil. Fry chicken until golden brown. Remove to roaster, 350 degree oven, or electric skillet. Add rest of ingredients. Simmer for about one hour. Add more Worcestershire sauce and wine if desired. If using the electric skillet you might put chicken on roaster tray if you do not want the chicken too brown.

SKILLET BARBECUED CHICKEN

> ½ fryer
> Salt and pepper to taste
> Oil to fry chicken
> Barbecue sauce (See Page 105)

Salt and pepper tender fryer. Cook in covered skillet for about 15 minutes on one side, in moderately hot oil. Remove cover. Turn pieces and fry on other side until brown. Pour off oil, but leave browned bits. Pour barbecue sauce over chicken. Cover. Simmer for about 15 minutes, turn, and pour sauce on other side. Simmer for at least 15 minutes more in order to let the flavors mingle.

THYME AND WINE CHICKEN

½ fryer
Flour to coat chicken
½ cup olive oil
Lemon juice to flavor
Salt and pepper to taste
Thyme
½ cup wine, white preferred

Salt and pepper chicken to taste. Flour chicken well. Place in skillet with heated olive oil. Sprinkle generously with thyme. Brown chicken on both sides. Squeeze or sprinkle lemon juice on each piece of chicken. Pour wine in pan. Cover and cook slowly until done and wine has been absorbed, usually about 45 minutes to 1 hour. Serve hot or cold.

ALUMINUM WRAPPED CHICKEN

Number of pieces of chicken desired
Butter
Salt and pepper to taste

Tightly seal seasoned chicken in aluminum foil. Place in shallow pan. Bake in 250 degree oven for 40 minutes or until done. Serve hot or cold.

Or: Instead of butter use French dressing.

Or: Instead of butter use Italian dressing and paprika to taste.

Or: Instead of butter sprinkle with parsley flakes, dehydrated onion, and hickory smoke salt. Baste with barbecue sauce.

fish
and
shellfish

Packaged frozen foods must have been invented with the "eating alone" person in mind. With few exceptions, you can buy almost any type of fish any time of the year at the frozen food counter. You can always remove the amount needed and keep the balance frozen until you want to eat it again. Directions for serving are on all packages. You can find sauces to serve with frozen or fresh fish on page 103.

PAN-FRIED FISH

Individual serving of fresh or frozen fish fillets
Salad oil to cover bottom of skillet

Sauté fish until golden brown on underside. Turn carefully. Sauté only until golden brown on underside, moist, and easily flaked. Do not overcook.

CANNED TUNA ON TOAST

½ can tuna. Freeze other half for use later.

[86]

½ cup white sauce
¼ tsp. oregano
  Pepper to taste
  Parsley
¼ cup grated cheese
½ onion minced

Simmer onions in tuna oil. Mix all ingredients. Brown toast on one side. Put mixture on unbrowned side. Broil in oven until brown on top.

CANNED FISH CROQUETTES (CODFISH, SALMON, OR TUNA)

1 6½ oz. can undrained tuna, salmon, or codfish
1 cup soft bread crumbs
1 TBS. minced onions
1 TBS. chopped parsley
1 tsp. lemon juice
⅛ tsp. pepper
½ tsp. salt
1 egg, beaten
1 TBS. cooking oil
  Cracker crumbs
  Cooking oil for frying deep enough to cover croquettes.

Bone fish. Stir in bread crumbs. Add beaten egg, all seasoning, and 1 TBS. cooking oil. Mix. Shape into 5 croquettes. Roll in cracker crumbs. Fry in fat deep enough to cover croquettes. Fry about 4 minutes on each side. Serve hot or cold. If sauce is desired, see page 103. Leftover croquettes are delicious for sandwiches or just a bite to eat when you get home after a busy day.

ITALIAN BROILED SHRIMP

This recipe will serve two or three people. However, it is one of my favorite recipes and I couldn't resist including it in this book.

> 1 lb. jumbo shrimp
> 2 TBS. olive oil
> 2 TBS. butter
> ½ cup drawn butter sauce
> 1 TBS. finely chopped garlic
> 2 TBS. finely chopped parsley
> 2 TBS. flour

Wash and shell shrimp, leaving tails on. (DO NOT COOK BEFOREHAND). Remove veins. Wash again in cold water and dry. Dust with flour. Put olive oil and butter in flat baking dish and heat under low broiler until butter is melted. Place shrimp in baking dish. Broil under low heat for 8 minutes. Add garlic and parsley to drawn butter sauce (below). Pour over broiled shrimp and stir until all shrimp are coated. Return to broiler and broil under high heat for 2 to 3 minutes. Serve immediately. Serves 2 to 3.

DRAWN BUTTER SAUCE. Melt 1 TBS. butter, add 1 TBS. flour, ¼ tsp. freshly ground pepper, ½ tsp. salt. ½ tsp. lemon juice, and 1 cup hot water. Bring to a boil, stirring constantly. Cook for 5 minutes. Add another 1 TBS. of butter and stir until melted. Salt and pepper seasoning can be changed to suit taste. Note: Use sauce as soon as prepared for best results.

OYSTER COCKTAIL

6 oysters
Sauce. See page 102.

PANNED OYSTERS

6 oysters
1 TBS. butter
Salt and pepper to taste
1 slice hot toast
Parsley

Place oysters in small saucepan and cook in their own liquid until edges begin to curl. Add butter, salt, and pepper. Serve oysters on toast. Garnish with parsley.

SHRIMP COCKTAIL

6 jumbo shrimp
Sauce. See page 106.

HOT SPICY SHRIMP

½ lb. raw unshelled shrimp
½ qt. boiling water
1 TBS. salt
½ TBS. pickling spice

Wash shrimp. Put in saucepan with rest of ingredients. Boil uncovered 15 minutes. Remove from heat. Let stand about 20 minutes in liquid. Serve shrimp unshelled. See page 101 for sauces to use.

CURRIED CRAB

1 6 oz. can crab meat, or use fresh crab
½ tsp. salt
¾ tsp. curry powder
3 TBS. salad oil
½ onion, cut in rings
⅓ cup chopped green pepper
2 medium tomatoes, cut in slim wedges

Pick over crab meat and remove small bones. Add salt and curry powder to crab meat. Sauté onion rings and pepper in hot oil in large heavy skillet. Add tomato wedges and crab meat. Cook 4 or 5 minutes more. Stir occasionally. When tomato and crab meat are heated through, serve.

vegetables

On page 98 you will find a cooking chart for fresh vegetables.

Of course, it is much easier to open a can of vegetables and heat quickly. The small cans are more than sufficient for one serving. Directions are always on the can.

As for frozen vegetables, they are much more interesting. You can easily cut the package in two and three sections and keep the balance frozen. Or you can cook the whole package, use as much as you want, and store the rest in your refrigerator. Most vegetables will keep for a week after cooking— that is, if you do not have sauces on them.

Sauces on page 101 can be fun to prepare and fun to eat.

Below are a few ideas in preparing vegetables of different types.

CANNED KIDNEY BEANS

¼ cup minced onion
1 TBS. butter
½ No. 2 can kidney beans

⅛ tsp. dried rosemary
¼ tsp. salt
2½ TBS. burgundy wine

Sauté onions until tender in butter. Add remaining ingredients. Simmer uncovered. Stir occasionally, and simmer about 15 minutes.

CHILI BEANS

½ No. 2 can kidney beans
1 to 2 TBS. chili powder
¾ cup water

Drain beans. Rinse in water. Put beans, chili powder, and water in saucepan. Simmer slowly for about 25 minutes or until beans taste as "chili-like" as you want.

GREEN BEANS

1 serving cooked green beans
½ tsp. caraway seeds
1 tsp. prepared cheese spread, any type

Drain beans which have been heated. Top with cheese and caraway seeds. Cover and let steam melt cheese slightly.

MARINATED GREEN BEANS

1 cup green beans, cooked
Cooking oil
Lemon juice
3 very thin slices onion
Salt and pepper to taste

Combine above ingredients. Chill well until ready to serve.

PANNED CURRIED CABBAGE

1½ cups finely shredded cabbage
¼ tsp. minced garlic
½ TBS. butter or salad oil
¼ tsp. curry powder
¼ tsp. salt

Sauté garlic in butter in skillet for 2 minutes. Stir in curry, cabbage, and salt. Cook, covered, for about 10 minutes. Stir occasionally.

EGGPLANT (See Eggplant Caviar, Page 159)

BLACK-EYED PEAS

1 cup black-eyed peas, frozen, fresh, or canned
1 TBS. diced onion

About 15 minutes before done, add onion.

MINT PEAS

½ or ⅓ package frozen peas
Dry mint leaves (flakes)
Water
Salt

Place ¼ cup water and ½ tsp. salt in small casserole. Add frozen peas and a few mint leaves. Cover and heat in oven until peas are tender.

PIMIENTO PEAS

Green peas, frozen, fresh, or canned
Pimiento, finely chopped

When ready to serve peas, add pimiento.

SPINACH

1 7½ oz. can spinach
   Lemon to taste

Cool spinach or heat spinach according to desire. Cut as finely as possible. Add lemon juice. Serve.

CASSEROLE SQUASH

This recipe makes four servings. Perhaps you have a neighbor you want to be nice to . . . so you can give her or him half of it. This dish is so delicious I couldn't keep from including it.

1 lb. yellow squash
1 small onion
1 tsp. salt
¼ cup water
   Pepper to taste
2 TBS. butter
1 egg
1 large slice bread, dried and crumbed.
½ cup grated cheese

Wash squash and cut into pieces. Cook squash and onion in salted water for about 20 minutes or until done. Remove from fire and let cool. Add egg and crumbs. Beat all ingredients with egg beater. Place in casserole and top with grated cheese. Bake at 350 degrees for 30 minutes until bubbly and hot. Can be served hot or cold.

FRENCH FRIED ONIONS

Heated salad oil, 1½" deep
1 peeled large onion
¼ cup milk
¼ cup flour
¼ tsp. salt

Heat salad oil in deep small saucepan over low heat. Slice onion ¼" thick. Separate into rings. Dip in milk and then in combined flour and salt. Fry a few at a time until light brown. Drain on brown paper.

HERBED FRIED ONIONS

2 medium onions
¼ TBS. butter
½ TBS. olive oil
Salt and pepper to taste
Pinch marjoram
Pinch cayenne pepper

Slice onion into ¼" slices. Heat butter and olive oil. Add onions, salt, pepper, marjoram, and cayenne. Stir until onions are moistened with fat. Cover. Cook over fairly slow heat ten to fifteen minutes, or until onions are tender. Add more salt if needed.

ITALIAN BROCCOLI

½ package frozen broccoli
Parmesan cheese
1½ TBS. olive oil

Cook broccoli until almost tender. Drain. Sauté in hot olive oil until delicately browned. Sprinkle with Parmesan cheese.

MARINATED ASPARAGUS

½ package frozen asparagus
Olive oil
Lemon juice
Salt and pepper

Cook asparagus until tender. Drain. Put in serving dish. Add olive oil to moisten and as much lemon juice as desired. Salt and pepper to taste. Chill until ready to serve.

BAKED SWEET POTATO

Wrap one sweet potato in aluminum foil. Bake in hot oven 35–45 minutes, or until tender when tested with a fork.

BAKED WHITE POTATO

Wrap one white potato in aluminum foil. Bake in hot oven 45–60 minutes, or until tender when tested with a fork.

STUFFED BAKED POTATO

After baked white potato is done, carefully remove from foil. Slice off top. Using knife, cut slashes in potato until crumbly. Add butter, salt and pepper to taste. Then mash

inside of potato with fork. Recover with slashed off top.
Place back in foil and reheat for a few moments.

Or: When adding ingredients, crumble about one tsp. of any
type of cheese.

Or: Add parsley leaves.

Or: Add chive tops or onion tops to taste.

FRENCH FRIED POTATOES

1 potato
Cooking oil

Wash and pare potato. In small saucepan heat salad oil, about
½ of saucepan. Over low heat, heat oil until about 385 degrees. Cut potato into about ¾" slices. Rinse in cold water.
Dry between towels. Fry potatoes from 20 to 30 minutes, or
until tender.

BAKED TOMATO

1 ripe medium tomato
¼ tsp. prepared mustard
1 tsp. minced onion
½ tsp. Worcestershire sauce
Salt
1 TBS. buttered soft bread crumbs

Heat oven to 375 degrees. Cut out stem end of tomato and
halve it, crosswise. Arrange cut side up in small baking pan.
Spread halves with mustard, top with minced onion and
Worcestershire sauce. Sprinkle with salt and crumbs. Bake
about 30 minutes.

APPROXIMATE TIME TABLE FOR COOKING
MARKET OR GARDEN VEGETABLES

Since frozen vegetables and canned vegetables are so easily bought the year round, it is time consuming to prepare market or garden vegetables. Also, fresh vegetables tend to lose flavor when cooked in small amounts. But for those of you who love fresh vegetables, and love to eat them in quantity, this table is included.

VEGETABLE	Before cooking, wash all vegetables thoroughly in lukewarm water.	*Approximate Cooking Time* Put 1" boiling water in saucepan. Add ½ tsp. salt for each cup. Add vegetables, cover and boil, as indicated.
Artichoke, French or Italian	Remove outside bottom leaves. Trim stems. Trim off brown or thorny leaf tops.	45–60 min.
Artichoke, Jerusalem	Pare thinly. Leave whole, dice, or slice.	15–35 min.
Asparagus	Break off stalks. Remove scales. Scrub well with soft brush to clean.	Use 9" or 10" skillet. Place asparagus in it. Boil in 1" boiling salted water. Cover. Boil 12–15 min.
Beans, Snap and Wax Green	Remove ends and string. Snap into 1" and 2" pieces. Cut crosswise. Cut lengthwise.	15–30 min. 10–20 min. 10–20 min.
Beans, Green Lima	Remove beans from pods.	20–30 min.
Beets—Young Old Young or Old	Leave whole with 1" stem. Leave whole with 1" stem. Pared. Sliced, diced, or slivered.	½ to 1 hr. 1–2 hrs. 20–30 min.
Broccoli	Remove large leaves and tough lower stalks. Pare tough skin off main stalks. Split each stalk in halves or quarters. Make several gashes along stalks.	Use 9" or 10" skillet. Place broccoli in it. Boil in 1" boiling salted water. Cover. Boil 15–20 min.

VEGETABLE	Before cooking, wash all vegetables thoroughly in lukewarm water.	*Approximate Cooking Time* Put 1" boiling water in saucepan. Add ½ tsp. salt for each cup. Add vegetables, cover and boil, as indicated.
Brussels Sprouts	Remove wilted leaves. Cut off bit of stem.	10–25 min.
Cabbage		
Green and Savoy	Shred fine.	5–8 min.
Green and Savoy	Cut in wedges.	8–12 min.
Red	Shred fine.	15–25 min.
Chinese	Shred fine.	4–5 min.
Carrots	Scrape or pare.	
	Sliced crosswise	6–20 min.
	Cut in thin slivers.	10–14 min.
	Quartered.	12–20 min.
	Cut in halves.	15–25 min.
	Whole.	20–40 min.
Cauliflower	Remove outer leaves and stalks:	
	Whole.	15–18 min.
	Broken in flowerets.	8–10 min.
Celery	Diced or slivered.	15–20 min.
Corn-on-cob	Remove husks and silk.	Cover corn with boiling water. Add ½ tsp. salt for each cup. Cover. Boil 5–6 min.
Greens:		
Beet Tops	If greens very young and tender, cook, covered, in water clinging to leaves after washing. Or, add ½" boiling water. Add ½ tsp. salt per each lb. of greens.	5–15 min.
Dandelion Greens		10–20 min.
Mustard Greens		7–10 min.
Spinach		6–10 min.
Swiss Chard, Young		3–10 min.
Turnip Greens		8–15 min.
Okra	Cut off stem end. Leave whole.	7–12 min.
Onions	Peel thin as possible.	
	Small whole, white.	23–25 min.
	2" medium.	28–30 min.
	¼" slices.	10 min.
Parsnips	Pare. Halve. Cut out center core. Cut in quarters.	7–15 min.

VEGETABLE	Before cooking, wash all vegetables thoroughly in lukewarm water.	*Approximate Cooking Time* Put 1″ boiling water in saucepan. Add ½ tsp. salt for each cup. Add vegetables, cover and boil, as indicated.
Peas	Remove peas from pods.	8–25 min. Add 1 tsp. sugar.
Potatoes		
Sweet	Whole, with skins.	30–35 min.
White	Mature or New. Whole, with skins, or pared thinly.	35–40 min.
	Mature, or New. Cut up.	20–25 min.
Pumpkin	Halve. Remove seeds and stringy part. Pare. Cut in 3″ pieces.	25–30 min.
Squash		
Acorn	Halve. Remove seeds and stringy part.	25 min.
Hubbard	Halve. Remove seeds and stringy part. Cut in small pieces.	25–30 min.
Summer		
Mature	Pare and seed. Cut in ½″ slices.	15–20 min.
Young	Cut in ½″ slices.	15–20 min.
Swiss Chard, Mature	Cut stalks from leaves.	
	Stalks, cut in 2″ pieces.	15 min.
	Leaves, in ½″ boiling salted water.	10 min.
Turnips	Pare thinly.	
White	Cut in ¼″ slices.	9–12 min.
	Cut in strips or ½″ cubes.	15–20 min.
Yellow	Cut in 2″ pieces.	35–40 min.
	Cut in strips or ½″ cubes.	20–25 min.
Zucchini	Cut in ½″ slices.	15–20 min.

sauces for meat, fish, and vegetables

You will find these sauces those most commonly used for fish, meat, and vegetables. The fun of preparing sauces is that they seem to invite you to experiment with added ingredients of your own choice, such as herbs, spices, and manufactured sauces. I would suggest that if you think you are going to perform a miracle with your experimentation, write down the ingredients as you go along. If it proves successful, you will have your personal addition to your sauce recipes.

Don't start tasting your sauce too soon. Give the ingredients the chance to ripen before adding too many extras.

GARLIC BUTTER

   1 clove garlic
      Salt and pepper
   1 to 1½ TBS. creamed butter
  ½ tsp. Worcestershire sauce
  ½ tsp. chopped basil

Crush garlic with 1 tsp. salt and beat into the creamed butter.
Add salt and pepper to taste, sauce, and chopped basil. Excellent with broiled fish or steak.

PLAIN MAYONNAISE

    1 egg
       Salt
       Cayenne pepper
    1 TBS. vinegar
    1 cup salad oil
       Little milk, if needed

Put egg in bowl with salt, cayenne pepper, and vinegar. Beat
oil in quickly. If too thick, dilute with a little milk.

QUICK COCKTAIL SAUCE

    Highly seasoned catsup
    Curry mustard

Combine as much as needed. Delicious for oyster or shrimp
cocktail.

COCKTAIL SAUCE

    1 TBS. tomato catsup
    ½ TBS. lemon juice
    ¼ tsp. salt
    3 to 4 drops hot sauce
    1 tsp. horse-radish
    ¼ tsp. Worcestershire sauce

Combine ingredients. Serve with raw oysters or shrimp cocktail.

HERB SAUCE FOR SHRIMP

1 TBS. salad oil
1 TBS. tarragon vinegar
¼ TBS. minced chives or green onion tops
¼ TBS. minced parsley
  Salt and pepper to taste
⅛ tsp. paprika
⅛ tsp. oregano

Mix ingredients. Chill to give flavors chance to mingle. Serve as dip or sauce for shrimp.

FISH FILLET SAUCE

Butter
Minced chives
Parsley

Combine and spread on fish while cooking or baking.

TARTAR SAUCE

¼ cup mayonnaise
¼ tsp. grated onion
⅛ cup finely chopped dill pickle
1 tsp. parsley

Mix ingredients. Serve with fish, seafood, or cucumbers.

Or: Add ½ tsp. chopped capers, few drops onion juice, and ¼ tsp. celery salt to above ingredients.

WHITE SAUCE

White sauce can be used for creaming cooked meat, flaked fish, and cooked vegetables. There are so many variations, I will not attempt to list them for you here. Below is a good basic recipe for ½ cup sauce:

    1 TBS. butter or cooking oil
    1 TBS. flour
    ½ cup milk
      Salt and pepper to taste
      Pinch paprika, if desired

Melt butter or heat cooking oil in small saucepan. Stir in flour and cook until mixture bubbles. Remove from heat and stir in milk slowly. Return to heat, stirring constantly. Add seasoning. Boil about 3 more minutes or until mixture has desired thickness.

Or: If using with plain fish fillets, add anchovy paste.

CHEESE SAUCE

      White sauce above
    ¼ cup shredded cheese
    ¼ tsp. Worcestershire sauce

After white sauce has thickened, add cheese and sauce. Stir over low heat until melted. Excellent for fish, meat, or any vegetables.

HOLLANDAISE SAUCE

1 egg yolk
⅛ tsp. salt
  Dash cayenne pepper
¼ cup melted butter
¼ TBS. lemon juice

Beat egg yolk until thick. Add salt and cayenne. Add half of melted butter, slowly. Beat constantly. Combine remaining butter with lemon juice and slowly add, about 1 tsp. at a time. Beat after each addition. Very tasty with most vegetables. Use portion needed. Chill balance. When balance needed for another serving, stir until soft over *lukewarm* water.

HAM MUSTARD SAUCE

⅛ tsp. prepared mustard
½ tsp. brown sugar

For ½ lb. slice ham, 1″ thick. After ham is brown on both sides, spread each side with above mixture. Continue frying until ham is done. Add more sauce if necessary.

BARBECUE SAUCE

4 TBS. oil
6 TBS. chopped onion
6 TBS. catsup
6 TBS. water
2 TBS. and 2 tsp. lemon juice
1½ TBS. brown sugar
1½ TBS. Worcestershire sauce
1 TBS. prepared mustard

1 tsp. salt
¼ tsp. pepper

Sauté onion in oil until tender. Add remaining ingredients. Simmer for about 15 minutes. Makes 1 cup. Unused portion can be kept in refrigerator for some time. This sauce can be used on hamburgers, broilers, pork, or lamb.

REMOULADE SAUCE FOR SHRIMP SALAD OR COCKTAIL

½ cup mayonnaise
½ clove garlic, minced fine
½ tsp. dry mustard
1½ TBS. parsley
½ tsp. chopped tarragon leaves
½ hard-cooked egg
8 capers

Combine above ingredients. In order to let the flavors mingle, it is suggested that this sauce be prepared 24 hours ahead of time, although it can be used immediately. Store unused portion in refrigerator.

rice

When cooking for one, it is most practical to use pre-cooked rice. There are many recipes on the packages, and by using the chart below you can prepare as much as you wish. Instead of using the often-called-for tomato juice or sauce, you can substitute water and bouillon cubes when you want to "pep up" your rice.

FOR ONE OR AMPLE ONE SERVING

Pre-Cooked Rice	Salt	Water	Makes
⅓ cup	dash	⅓ cup	⅔ cup
⅔ cup	¼ tsp.	⅔ cup	1-⅓ cup

CURRIED PRE-COOKED RICE

½ cup pre-cooked rice (makes 1 cup cooked)
½ cup water
½ tsp. curry powder
 1 bouillon cube
  Chopped onion
  Salad oil or butter to cover bottom of pan

Brown onions and rice in salad oil or butter. Add rest of

ingredients. Bring to boil. Simmer 5 to 7 minutes. Turn off heat. Cover.

MEXICAN RICE

¼ TBS. cooking oil
¼ cup raw rice
¼ onion, minced
 1 TBS. green pepper, chopped
¼ tsp. salt
¼ tsp. chili powder
¼ cup tomatoes, finely cut up, or canned tomatoes
¼ cup water

Wash rice well and dry. Brown raw rice in cooking oil. Add onion, green pepper, salt, chili powder, and tomatoes. Mix well and add just enough water to cover mixture. Cover with lid and allow to simmer until rice is tender, about 30 minutes. Remove lid to allow mixture to dry out. DO NOT STIR after the cooking starts as the mixture will become gummy.

SPANISH RICE (See Page 168)

WILD RICE

As you know, wild rice is rather expensive, but since you can always store the uncooked rice in box in a plastic bag in the refrigerator—as you can store other foods—here is one recipe:

¼ cup wild rice (makes ¾ cup)
¼ tsp. salt
 3 cups boiling water

Rinse wild rice *well* in cold water. Add rice slowly to boiling salted water. Cover. Stir occasionally. Boil 25 or 30 minutes, or until tender. Drain. Add butter.

Or: Add ¾ TBS. chopped green onion tops or chives.

desserts

Let's have guests! What better excuse can you use to defy our calorie-conscious world. Now you can indulge in desserts for a cause! I have tried to include a little bit of everything —so, be tempted! All these recipes are of average size so your guests can be included.

BAKED APPLES

    Apples, as many as needed
1 TBS. sugar
¼ tsp. cinnamon
    Syrup, or 4 TBS. butter mixed with 1 cup sugar and 1 TBS. water

Wash apples, remove cores and blemishes. Score around middle, just enough to cut skin. Put apples into pan and fill each center with 1 TBS. sugar mixed with ¼ tsp. cinnamon. Pour syrup over all apples. Bake in hot oven 30 to 40 minutes or until tender.

SPICED APRICOTS

1 lb. dried apricots (unsoaked)
2 cups water

3 or 4 whole cloves
½ cup sugar
½ tsp. cinnamon

Wash apricots. Place in two quart baking dish. Add sugar, water, and spice. Cover. Bake in medium oven about 1 hour and 15 minutes.

FRIED BANANAS

2 bananas, large
1 box corn flakes, small
Cream
Butter

Slice bananas, lengthwise and crosswise. Dip in cream and then corn flakes. Fry in butter until light brown. If desired pour warmed brandy over bananas, ignite, and serve.

BUTTERSCOTCH PEACH CRISP

½ cup brown sugar, firmly packed
½ cup flour
⅛ tsp. cinnamon
Dash of nutmeg
¼ cup butter or margarine
1 can sliced peaches

Mix sugar, flour and spices. Cut in butter. Drain peaches and place in greased baking dish. Sprinkle sugar mixture over them and bake 25 minutes in moderate oven heated to 375 degrees.

STRAWBERRY FROST

½ pint ripe strawberries
¼ cup sugar
½ cup milk
2 TBS. cream
1 TBS. lemon juice
½ tsp. vanilla
  Pinch salt
  Vanilla ice cream

Combine strawberries, sugar, and milk. Beat with rotary egg beater until creamy. Gradually add milk and cream, beating after each addition. Beat in lemon juice, vanilla, and salt. Into each chilled glass put 1 or 2 scoops vanilla ice cream. Fill with strawberry mixture. Garnish with strawberries.

BANANA PUDDING

2 egg yolks
1 egg
½ cup sugar
1½ TBS. flour
3 cups milk
4 or 5 bananas
  Vanilla wafers

Combine eggs, sugar, flour and milk. Slice bananas and cover bottom of cooking dish. Cover with layer of vanilla wafers. Pour mixture over. Bake in moderate oven until liquid is thick.

BAKED LEMON PUDDING

    1 cup sugar
    3 TBS. flour
    1 cup milk
    2 eggs, separated
      Juice of 1 lemon

Combine sugar, flour, milk, beaten egg yolks, and juice of lemon. Fold in beaten egg whites. Pour in buttered pyrex loaf pan which is centered in pan of hot water. Bake at 350 degrees for about 30 minutes.

CHOCOLATE NUT BREAD PUDDING

    2 slices lightly buttered bread, cubed or whole
    1 cup milk
    1 egg
    2 TBS. sugar
    ⅛ tsp. salt
    ¼ tsp. vanilla extract
    ¼ cup chocolate bits (or 2 TBS. cocoa with sugar)
    2 TBS. chopped nuts

Place bread in baking dish. Beat eggs, milk, sugar and salt together. Add chocolate bits and nuts. Pour over bread. Add vanilla. Place dish in pan of hot water and bake about 40 minutes or until firm in center.

PINEAPPLE TRIFLE

    1 pkg. orange flavored gelatin
    1 cup boiling water
      Drained juice from can pineapple and orange.
      (Add water to fill one cup.)

1 cup canned grated pineapple, drained
1 orange, free from membrane, cut in pieces and drained
½ cup cream, whipped
½ cup sugar

Dissolve gelatin in boiling water. Add fruit juice and water. Chill. When slightly thickened, beat with rotary egg beater until consistency of whipped cream. Fold in fruit and whipped cream, to which sugar has been added. Turn into freezing tray of refrigerator. Chill 1½ to 2 hours. Serve in slices.

WINE JELLY

2 packages gelatin
½ cup water
1 cup sugar
1⅔ cups water
⅓ cup orange juice
3 TBS. lemon juice
1 cup sherry

Dissolve gelatin in ½ cup water. Bring to boil 1⅔ cup water and 1 cup sugar. Add dissolved gelatin. Add rest of ingredients. Pour into molds, custard cups or a bowl. Chill until firm.

LEMON REFRIGERATOR CAKE

2 eggs
½ cup sugar
Rind and juice of 1 lemon

  1 cup heavy cream
  ⅔ cup graham cracker or vanilla wafer crumbs

Separate yolks from whites of eggs and mix yolks with sugar, lemon rind, and juice. Cook over hot, not boiling water, until thick as heavy cream. Stir constantly. Remove from heat and cool.

Beat egg whites until they stand in points. In a separate bowl beat heavy cream until it holds shape. Now stir the cool lemon mixture into the egg whites gently, then add the beaten cream lightly.

Sprinkle half of cracker or wafer crumbs over bottom of an ice-cube tray. Pour in dessert mixture and sprinkle remaining crumbs over the top. Place in refrigerator and freeze until firm for several hours. Serves 4.

PEPPERMINT ICE-CREAM CAKE

  10 inch angel cake. Can be made from mix.
   6 chocolate peppermint patties
  ½ cup nuts
   1 quart vanilla ice cream
  ⅛ tsp. peppermint extract

Cut cool angel cake into 4 layers. Chop up peppermint patties and nuts. Soften ice cream slightly and stir in candy, nuts, and peppermint extract. Spread thick layer of ice cream between cake layers and rebuild the cake. Cover top of cake with thick frosting of ice cream and keep in freezing compartment until firm. No thawing is necessary. Serves 6 to 8.

BANANA CAKE

    2 cups flour
 1½ cups sugar
  ½ cup butter
    2 eggs
    4 TBS. buttermilk
    1 tsp. soda
    3 crushed bananas
  ½ cup nuts, chopped
    1 tsp. vanilla

Cream butter and sugar. Add beaten eggs. Add buttermilk.
Add flour and soda sifted three times. Add crushed bananas,
vanilla and nuts. Pour in pan which has been greased only
on the bottom. Bake about 25 minutes in oven heated from
350 to 375 degrees.

COCOA CAKE

 1¼ cups flour
    1 cup sugar
    3 TBS. cocoa
    1 tsp. baking soda
  ⅛ tsp. salt
    2 eggs
    1 cup sour cream
    1 tsp. vanilla

Sift flour and then measure. Mix all dry ingredients together
and sift three times. Beat eggs, add cream and vanilla, and
then the sifted dry ingredients. Blend well. Bake in 9 inch

diameter pan, at least 2 inches deep, for 30 minutes at 350 degrees.

COFFEE CHIFFON CAKE

  2 eggs, separated
1½ cups sugar
2¼ cups sifted cake flour
  3 tsp. baking powder
  1 tsp. salt
  ½ cup milk
  ½ cup cold coffee
  ⅛ tsp. baking soda
  ⅓ cup cooking oil
  2 tsp. vanilla

Beat egg whites until frothy. Gradually beat in half cup of sugar. Continue beating until very stiff and glossy. Sift remaining sugar, flour, baking powder and salt into another bowl. Combine milk, coffee and baking soda. Pour oil into flour mixture with half the coffee mixture and vanilla. Beat 1 minute using medium speed on electric mixer or 150 strokes by hand. Scrape sides and bottom of bowl constantly. Add remaining coffee mixture and egg yolks. Beat 1 minute longer, scraping bowl constantly. Fold in egg white mixture lightly but thoroughly.

Pour into 2 deep well-greased and floured 8 inch layer cake pans. Bake in moderate oven at 350 degrees 30 to 35 minutes. Remove from pans and cool. Split each layer into 2 layers. Put together and frost with Fluffy Coffee Frosting (see page 120). Chill well

GELATIN CAKE

1 box white cake mix
4 eggs
¾ cup apricot nectar
1 box orange gelatin

Combine all ingredients well. Bake in loaf pan until done.

JELLY ROLL

3 eggs
1 cup sugar
2 TBS. milk
1 cup flour
1 tsp. baking powder
   Rind of 1 lemon, grated. Or ½ tsp. lemon extract.
   Tart jelly
   Powdered sugar

Beat egg yolks, sugar, and milk until very light. Add stiffly beaten egg whites and fold in flour in which baking powder has been sifted. Flavor with grated rind of lemon or ½ tsp. lemon extract. Bake in long shallow pan in moderate oven. Remove from pan while hot and place on a wet cloth. Spread with tart jelly and roll quickly. Sprinkle wax paper with powdered sugar and wrap it around jelly roll. Let stand until cool.

POPPY SEED CAKE

¾ cup milk
¾ cup poppy seed (2–2¼ oz. pkgs.)

> ¾ cup shortening
> 1½ cup sugar
> 1 tsp. vanilla
> 2 cups cake flour
> 2 tsp. baking powder
> ⅛ tsp. salt
> 4 egg whites

Sift dry ingredients. Soak milk and poppy seed overnight. Cream shortening and sugar. Add vanilla. Alternate milk and poppy seed mixture with dry ingredients into shortening and sugar. Fold in egg whites, beaten stiff. Pour into two 9 inch layer pans which are greased and floured. Bake at 325 degrees for 30 to 45 minutes or until cake leaves sides of pan.

Filling:

> 4 egg yolks
> 3 TBS. flour
> 1 cup sugar
> 2 cups milk

Combine all ingredients. Cook and stir constantly. When thick add vanilla. Cool. Spread between layers and over top and sides of cake.

STRAWBERRY SHORTCAKE

> ½ cup biscuit mix
> 1 tsp. sugar
> 1 TBS. cooking oil
> 2 to 3 TBS. milk
> Strawberries, sugared to taste

Make into 1 or 2 shortcake shapes. Bake in hot oven until brown or 10 to 12 minutes. Split and fill with strawberries. Serves 1.

UPSIDE DOWN CAKE

 1 TBS. butter
 ¼ cup brown sugar, packed solid
 6 canned pineapple slices, drained
 1¼ cups sifted cake flour
 1½ tsp. baking powder
 ¼ tsp. salt
 ¼ cup cooking oil
 ¾ cup granulated sugar
 1 egg, beaten
 ½ cup milk
 1 tsp. vanilla

Melt butter in pan 8 inches in diameter and 2 inches deep. Sprinkle well with brown sugar. Arrange pineapple slices, whole if possible, on brown sugar. Sift together cake flour, baking powder, and salt. Work in cooking oil until creamy. Slowly add granulated sugar until well dissolved. Add egg and beat mixture well. Alternately add flour, milk, and vanilla, stirring smooth after each addition. Spread on pineapple. Bake in moderate oven at 350 degrees 40 minutes or until done. Remove from oven. Let stand about 5 minutes. Loosen with spatula and cover pan with inverted serving plate. Turn over carefully. Lift off pan. Serves 6.

FLUFFY COFFEE FROSTING

 1½ cups vegetable shortening
 1 cup granulated sugar

½ tsp. salt
¼ cup cold coffee
1 tsp. vanilla
2 eggs

Combine all ingredients in small mixing bowl. If using an electric mixer, beat at high speed. If using rotary beater, beat for 10 minutes or until smooth and fluffy. (This frosting resembles that used in French pastries.)

WHITE COOKED ICING

2 cups sugar
¾ cup water
¼ tsp. cream of tartar
2 egg whites, beaten stiff
1 tsp. vanilla

Boil sugar, water, and cream of tartar until syrup spins into a thread. Pour hot syrup over beaten egg whites. Add vanilla. Beat until ready to spread.

WHITE UNCOOKED ICING

¼ cup shortening
2 cups confectioners' sugar, sifted
2 TBS. cream
1 tsp. vanilla

Blend shortening and sugar. Stir in cream and vanilla. Beat until ready to spread.

CHOCOLATE-PECAN SQUARES

    2 4-oz. pkgs. sweet cooking chocolate
    1 TBS. water
    4 beaten egg yolks
    2 TBS. sifted confectioners' sugar
    ½ cup pecans, chopped
    4 egg whites, beaten stiff
    1 6-oz. can evaporated milk, chilled icy cold and
      whipped
      Vanilla wafers

In double boiler melt chocolate with water. Remove from heat. Stir in egg yolks, then sugar. Cool to room temperature, then stir in pecans. Fold in egg whites and whipped evaporated milk. Cover bottom and sides of 8 x 8 x 2 inch baking dish with layer of vanilla wafers. Top with half of the chocolate mixture, then with layer of wafers. Carefully spoon on remaining chocolate. Trim with wafer halves. Chill several hours or overnight. Cut in 8 squares.

DROP TEA CAKES

    ½ cup shortening
    1 cup sugar
    ½ tsp. nutmeg
    ½ tsp. salt
    2 beaten eggs
    2 TBS. milk
      Rind of 1 lemon, grated
    2 cups sifted flour
    1 tsp. baking powder
    ½ tsp. soda
      Cinnamon and sugar, combined

Mix shortening, sugar, nutmeg, and salt. Combine milk and eggs and add to mixture. Add rind of lemon. Combine sifted flour, baking powder, and soda and add to mixture. Drop in small amounts on cookie sheet. Flatten with bottom of glass that is covered with a well-wrung wet cloth. Sprinkle combined sugar and cinnamon on cakes. Bake in oven heated to 350 degrees about 10 minutes. DO NOT OVERCOOK.

FILLED SANDTARTS

2¾ cup flour
½ lb. butter
4 TBS. sugar
½ tsp. plum butter or preserves or jelly for each tart
    Pecans, finely chopped

Sift flour and sugar. Blend in butter until dough is stiff. Roll in balls 1 inch in diameter. Stick finger in center and fill hole with ½ tsp. plum butter, preserves, or jelly. This action will flatten the tart. Dip both sides of tart in finely chopped pecans. Bake in about 300 degrees oven for 15 minutes or until golden brown. When cool, if desired, dip in powdered sugar.

SINGLE CRUST PASTRY

There are any number of excellent packaged pie crust mixes available at your favorite grocery store. For the times you want to try your hand at preparing the crust in your own kitchen, the recipe is given below:

1⅓ cups all-purpose flour, sifted
1 tsp. salt

⅓ cup cooking oil
3 TBS. whole milk, cold

Mix flour and salt. Pour cooking oil and milk into a cup without stirring. Add all at once to flour. Stir until mixed. Press into round ball, then flatten slightly. Place between two sheets of waxed paper. Roll out gently to size needed for pie pan. Remove top sheet of paper, carefully turn over dough and place in pie pan. Flute edge and prick thoroughly with fork. Bake in 475 degree oven (very hot) 8 to 10 minutes.

ANGEL FOOD PIE

1 9 inch baked pastry shell
4½ TBS. cornstarch
¾ cup sugar
1½ cups boiling water
⅜ tsp. salt
3 egg whites
3 TBS. sugar
1½ tsp. vanilla
½ cup cream, whipped
½ square bitter chocolate, grated. Or: nuts, grated

Mix cornstarch and sugar in a saucepan or top of double-boiler. Add boiling water, stirring constantly until thick and clear, about 10 to 12 minutes. Add salt to egg whites and beat until stiff. Add sugar and vanilla, beating until the egg whites are creamy. Pour hot cornstarch over the egg whites, beating continuously. Cool slightly and fill pie shell. Cover with whipped cream. Sprinkle grated chocolate or nuts on top. Chill at least 2 hours before serving.

CHERRY PIE

1 9 inch baked pastry shell, cooled
1 small pkg. cream cheese
1 cup powdered sugar
1 cup cream, whipped
1 can cherry pie filling

Mix cream and sugar well with fork. Add whipped cream. Pour in pastry shell. Top with cherry pie filling. Chill overnight or all day before serving.

CHOCOLATE VELVET

1 9 inch baked pastry shell, cooled
1 stick (1/4 lb.) margarine
3/4 cup sugar
1 square chocolate, melted
1 tsp. vanilla
2 eggs, chilled, unbeaten
Ice cream

USE ELECTRIC BEATER ONLY. Cream margarine and sugar. Add melted chocolate and vanilla. Add eggs, unbeaten, one at a time. Beat 2 minutes after each addition. Pour in shell and chill. Serve topped with ice cream.

STRAWBERRY CHIFFON PIE

1 9 inch baked pastry shell, cooled
1 pkg. strawberry chiffon pie filling mix
1/2 cup boiling water
1/2 cup cold drained strawberry juice

2 to 4 TBS. sugar
1 pkg. (10 oz.) quick frozen sliced strawberries, thawed and drained

Place contents of package in large deep mixing bowl. Add boiling water and mix thoroughly. Add drained strawberry juice. Then beat vigorously with a rotary beater, or at highest speed of electric mixer, until mixture is very foamy (about 1 minute). Add sugar and beat until filling stands in peaks (takes 1 to 3 minutes). Fold in drained strawberries. Pour into cooled pie shell. Chill about 2 hours or until set.

APPLE PIE

Cinnamon or nutmeg
3½ cups fresh apples
1 cup sugar
4 TBS. flour
1 TBS. butter
Single crust pastry recipe doubled (page 123)

Peel apples and core. Cut pieces of apple at least ½ inch thick. Combine sugar with flour and spread half of amount on bottom of pan which is lined with pastry WHICH HAS NOT BEEN PIERCED. Add apples and pour over balance of sugar. Sprinkle butter in tiny pieces. Add few dashes of cinnamon or nutmeg. Moisten edge of crust with water. Cover with top of crust and trim off top pastry 1 inch from edge of pan. Press edges together and then flute. Bake at 450 degrees for 20 minutes and then 400 degrees about 30 minutes.

PECAN PIE

½ cup granulated sugar
1 cup dark corn syrup
3 eggs
4 TBS. butter
1 TBS. vanilla extract
1 cup pecan meats, broken
Single crust pastry recipe

Combine sugar and syrup. Cook until mixture thickens. Beat eggs without separating and slowly add hot syrup to beaten eggs, beating constantly. Add butter, vanilla, and nuts. Pour into unbaked pie shell WHICH HAS NOT BEEN PIERCED. When cool serve with whipped cream or ice cream if desired. Bake in oven heated to 450 degrees for ten minutes and then reduce to 300 degrees for 35 minutes.

PUMPKIN PIE DESSERT

Crumb crust:

1½ cups graham crackers, crumbed
1 TBS. sugar
½ cup margarine, melted
Dash cinnamon

Combine and pack on pie tin. Bake at 350 degrees about 10 minutes. Cool.

Filling:

32 marshmallows, large
½ cup milk
1 cup pumpkin, canned

  ½ tsp. cinnamon
  ½ tsp. allspice
  1 cup cream, whipped or
    1 small can evaporated milk, whipped

Combine marshmallows and ½ cup milk in saucepan. Heat. Stir until marshmallows are melted. Remove from stove. Add pumpkin, cinnamon, and allspice. Fold in whipped cream. Pour in shell and chill.

MEXICAN CANDY (Pralines)

  1 cup sugar (⅔ white and ⅓ brown sugar)
  1 cup nuts, unchopped
  4 TBS. water

Combine. Cook until thickens or when drop of mixture dropped in cold water forms a ball. Beat a little. Pour tablespoonful of mixture at a time on wax paper.

HEAVENLY HASH MOUNDS

  1 6 oz. pkg. semi-sweet chocolate bits
  ½ cup nuts, broken or chopped (optional)
  2 TBS. white corn syrup
  1 cup miniature marshmallows
  1 TBS. water
  1 tsp. vanilla

Melt chocolate with syrup and water. Blend ingredients when chocolate has melted. Remove from heat and add nuts and marshmallows. Drop from teaspoon onto waxed paper. To cool quickly, place in refrigerator.

DR PEPPER PARTY PUNCH

1 cup sugar
6 lemons
6 limes
½ cup grenadine
6 bottles Dr Pepper
2 quarts chilled soda
2 trays Dr Pepper ice cubes (Pour Dr Pepper into ice trays instead of water)
1 cup cherries, with stems

Boil sugar in one cup of water, slowly, until sugar is dissolved. Cool. When cool add to strained juice of lemons and limes. Pour into chilled punch bowl. Stir in grenadine, Dr Pepper and sparkling water. Float cherries on top.

FRENCH MARTINI

8 jiggers gin
4 jiggers dry vermouth
½ jigger Crème de Cacao
1 jigger Kirsch

Mix in usual way. Serves four.

PLANTER'S PUNCH

1 jigger lime juice
2 jiggers simple syrup (made from 2 cups water and 1 cup sugar boiled until thick)
3 jiggers rum (light white)

Fill glasses with ice. Pour mixture over.

PUNCH

1 large can frozen orange juice with amount of water suggested on can
1 large can frozen limeade with amount of water suggested on can
1 #2 can pineapple juice
2 quarts ginger ale

Mix orange juice, limeade and pineapple juice with required water. Freeze a portion in a ring mold or other suitable container. This may be floated in punch bowl at serving time to keep punch cool without diluting punch mixture. When ready to serve, pour balance of mix and ginger ale in punch bowl. Add frozen mix.

Or: Instead of ginger ale, substitute vodka or champagne.

RAISIN WINE

1 lb. box raisins
2 cups sugar
½ gallon bottle
  Water

Rinse raisins well. Put raisins and sugar in ½ gallon bottle. Fill bottle with water until about 2 inches from top. Mix well until sugar is dissolved.

Screw lid on bottle loosely or bottle will explode.

Every 48 hours for first week press raisins below water level. If any raisins should mildew, remove such raisins. ALWAYS LEAVE SCREW LID LOOSE as raisins will be fermenting.

Let stand for at least 30 days before serving. Strain. Liquid may be returned to gallon bottle or put in smaller bottles. Continue to leave covers loose for another 30 days, or until wine becomes clearer. If desired, liquid can be strained again. After 60 days from time recipe was started covers on bottles can be tightened.

TEQUILA SALTY DOG

     1 tsp. simple syrup (sugar combined with water)
   ⅔ jigger lime or lemon juice
     2 jiggers tequila
       Mint
       Sprinkle of salt

Fill tall glasses with cracked ice. Pour syrup, lime, or lemon juice and tequila into glass. Add sparkling water. Sprinkle with salt and decorate with mint.

Or: Use gin instead of tequila.

VIENNESE COFFEE

   Brewed coffee, extra strength
   Cream, whipped

Sweeten coffee to taste. Top with whipped cream.

biscuits, muffins and breads

You will find that most of these recipes are in more than one serving size. They are included for you because so many people like to prepare their own breads for a change from the "store bought" variety. I know you will enjoy baking them.

PLAIN BISCUITS

    1   cup sifted all-purpose flour
  1½   tsp. baking powder
    ½   tsp. salt
  2½   TBS. cooking oil
    ⅓   cup milk

Heat oven very hot, about 475 degrees. Together sift flour, baking powder and salt. Pour cooking oil and milk into a measuring cup but do not blend. Pour all at once into flour. Stir with fork until dough rounds up into a ball. Smooth by kneading dough. Press out to desired thickness. Cut with unfloured cutter. Bake on ungreased cookie sheet, about 10 to 12 minutes. Makes about 8 medium biscuits.

DROP BISCUITS

Follow above recipe but do not smooth out. Drop dough from spoon on to ungreased cookie sheet. Bake 10 to 12 minutes. Makes about 8 medium biscuits.

CHEESE BISCUITS

   1 cup flour
   1 tsp. baking powder
   ½ tsp. salt
   2 TBS. shortening
   ¼ to ⅓ cup milk
   ½ tsp. butter
   2 oz. natural aged Cheddar cheese, cut in pieces

Combine flour, baking powder, and salt in bowl. Cut in shortening until mixture resembles coarse crumbs. Gradually work milk into flour mixture, adding enough to make a firm dough that is easy to handle.

Turn dough out on a lightly floured board. Roll out to about ½ inch thick. Cut dough with biscuit cutter and place in circles about ½ inch apart in shallow baking pan which has been lightly greased.

Meanwhile, melt butter with cheese over boiling water in double boiler. Stir frequently until well blended. Drizzle cheese mixture over biscuits in pan. Bake about 10 minutes or until golden brown at 450 degrees. Makes about 12 biscuits.

HAM AND CHEESE BISCUITS

Deviled ham (4½ oz. can)

Eight wedges of cheese
Plain biscuit recipe

Bake biscuits as in plain biscuit recipe. Remove from oven. Cover each biscuit generously with deviled ham. Top with wedges of cheese. Return to oven for 3 minutes. Serve hot. Makes 8.

MUFFINS

> 1 cup sifted all-purpose flour
> 1⅛ tsp. baking powder
> ½ tsp. salt
> 2½ TBS. sugar
> 1 small egg, beaten
> ½ cup milk
> 1 TBS. cooking oil

Heat oven very hot, about 475 degrees. Oil muffin pans. Sift dry ingredients together. Combine cooking oil, milk, and egg. Stir quickly into dry mixture until ingredients are just moist and batter still has lumpy appearance. Fill muffin pans ⅔ full. Bake about 20 minutes. Makes six muffins.

BLUEBERRY MUFFINS

> Muffin recipe
> ½ cup drained blueberries

Add drained blueberries to ingredients of muffin recipe. Follow baking instruction. Makes 6.

DATE MUFFINS

Muffin recipe
7 TBS. sliced dates

Add sliced dates to ingredients of muffin recipe. Follow baking instructions. Makes 6.

ORANGE BRAN MUFFINS

½ cup sifted flour
1½ tsp. double-acting baking powder
½ tsp. salt
1 to 2 TBS. sugar
3 TBS. shortening
1 egg, well beaten
⅓ cup orange juice
¾ cup (1 oz. pkg.) 40% bran flakes

Sift flour once. Measure, add baking powder, salt, and sugar and sift again. Cut in shortening. Combine egg and orange juice and add all at once to flour mixture. Mix. Add bran flakes and mix again slightly. Turn into greased muffin pans, filling them ⅔ full. Bake in hot oven (400 degrees) 30 minutes, or until done. Makes 6.

CORN MUFFINS

¼ cup sifted all-purpose flour
¼ tsp. soda
¾ tsp. baking powder
½ tsp. salt
1 TBS. sugar

⅔ cups cornmeal
1 small egg, beaten
⅔ cup buttermilk
2 TBS. cooking oil

Heat oven to 425 degrees (hot). Sift together all dry ingredients except cornmeal. Stir in cornmeal. Combine egg, buttermilk, and cooking oil. Add dry ingredients. Stir quickly until well mixed. Grease muffin tins and fill pans ⅔ full. Bake 12 to 15 minutes or until golden brown. Makes about 9 muffins.

CORN BREAD

1 cup sifted all-purpose flour
3 TBS. sugar, if desired
3 tsp. baking powder
1 tsp. salt
1 cup cornmeal
1 egg, beaten
¼ cup cooking oil
1¼ cups milk

Heat oven to 425 degrees (hot). Sift together flour, sugar, baking powder, and salt. Stir in cornmeal. Combine egg, cooking oil, and milk. Add to dry ingredients and mix quickly. Turn into oiled 11 x 7 x 2-inch pan. Bake 30 minutes. Makes 12 squares.

SKILLET CORN BREAD

Corn bread recipe

Prepare corn bread recipe. Heat skillet, oil slightly. Pour

ingredients into skillet. Cover. Cook over low heat 30 to 35 minutes until done. Turn out on platter.

CORN STICKS

Corn bread recipe

Prepare corn bread recipe. Heat corn stick pans in oven. Remove carefully and brush well with cooking oil. Fill hot pans ⅔ full with mixture of corn bread. Bake at 425 degrees 15 to 20 minutes, or until golden brown. Makes 14 large sticks.

POPOVERS

    ⅔ cup sifted all-purpose flour
    ⅛ tsp. salt
    ½ cup milk
    1 egg

Sift flour and salt into bowl. Combine milk and well beaten egg. Stir gradually into dry ingredients until batter is smooth. Beat thoroughly with egg beater. Into piping hot, well greased popover pans, or deep muffin tins, pour mixture until ⅔ full. Bake about 50 minutes or until done. Makes 6.

WAFFLES

The frozen waffles on the market today are very tasty. However, we all sometimes wish for a taste of the old-fashioned waffle started from scratch in your own kitchen.

    1 cup flour
    ¼ tsp. salt
    2 tsp. baking powder
    1 TBS. sugar

About 1 cup milk
1 egg
3 TBS. melted shortening or cooking oil

Sift flour. Measure and sift again with salt, baking powder, and sugar. Beat eggs until light. Add milk and shortening or cooking oil. Add sifted dry ingredients. Mix only enough to moisten ingredients.

Or: Add ¼ cup chopped nut meats to batter.

Or: Add ½ cup drained pineapple to batter.

Or: Add ½ cup chopped ham.

Or: Add ½ cup chopped dates.

PANCAKES

There are any number of excellent pancake mixes on the market to which you only add milk or water. The "do-it-yourself" recipe hunter will like the one below:

1 cup sifted all-purpose flour
3 tsp. baking powder
2 TBS. sugar
½ tsp. salt
1 egg
1 cup milk
2 TBS. cooking oil

Sift dry ingredients. To beaten egg add milk and cooking oil. Add dry ingredients. Beat to a fairly smooth batter. Makes five 6-inch pancakes.

Or: Pour pancake batter over short strips of crisp bacon. Serve bacon side up.

FRENCH TOAST

1 egg, slightly beaten
About ¼ cup milk
⅛ tsp. salt
⅔ tsp. sugar, granulated
2 slices bread, cut in halves or quarters

Combine egg, milk, salt and sugar. Heat cooking oil in skillet. Dip the bread in egg mixture, quickly, and fry over low heat, browning on both sides.

Or: Instead of using granulated sugar, substitute cinnamon sugar.

CHOCOLATE DOUGHNUTS

1½ TBS. shortening
⅔ cup sugar
1 egg, beaten
¼ tsp. soda
1 tsp. baking powder
½ tsp. cinnamon
½ tsp. salt
1 cup sour milk
2½ cups flour
5 squares chocolate, melted in double boiler

Cream shortening, egg, and sugar. Sift dry ingredients. Add melted chocolate to shortening, egg and sugar. Combine with milk and soda and then add to dry ingredients. Roll out. Cut with doughnut cutter. Fry until done in about 1½ inches of cooking oil in skillet heated hot. Doughnuts are usually done in 1 to 2 minutes.

CARROT BREAD

¾ cup cooking oil
1 cup sugar
1½ cup flour
1 tsp. soda
1 tsp. cinnamon
¼ tsp. salt
1 cup grated carrots
2 eggs
½ cup pecans
½ tsp. vanilla

Mix the ingredients as listed. Beat eggs slightly before adding to mixture. Pour in greased and floured loaf pan. Bake at 325 degrees for 1 hour and 15 minutes or until done.

GARLIC BREAD

There are many ways to prepare garlic bread, depending on how much bread you are going to eat.

For one: Butter slices of bread, brush garlic juice lightly over butter and toast in oven or broiler. For stronger flavor sprinkle with garlic button chopped fine.

For a crowd: Using a French loaf, rub entire outside crust with garlic. Slice bread about ¾ through crosswise. Brush with melted butter (to which more garlic may be added if desired). Sprinkle with grated Parmesan cheese and dehydrated parsley. Sprinkle paprika lightly. Place in oven until hot and crisp. Or wrap in aluminum foil and place in hot oven until ready to serve.

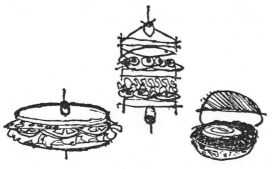

sandwiches

Most of these sandwiches are for one. Here you will also find some recipes for some super "out-size" sandwiches. The "out-size" sandwiches can be prepared on those days when you are extra hungry.

COLD MEAT SANDWICH

Slice meat, any type
Thin slices of tomato
Thin slices dill or sweet pickle
Salt and pepper to taste
Mayonnaise

Spread bread with mayonnaise. Add remaining ingredients in layers.

HAMBURGER

No cookbook would be complete without THE hamburger. This recipe seems to be the most popular.

¼ lb. ground beef pattie, mashed slightly larger than
       bun to be used
     Salt and pepper to taste
1 slice onion
1 slice tomato
2 slices dill pickle
1 lettuce leaf
     Mustard
     Bun, toasted or untoasted

Salt and pepper pattie and fry to desired doneness. Place on
bottom half of bun. Spread meat with mustard. Add onion,
tomato, pickle and lettuce leaf. Cover with top half of bun.
Top half of bun can also be spread with mustard if desired.

HAM AND CHEESE ON RYE

1 slice ham
1 slice cheese, Swiss or American
     Hot mustard

Spread mustard on buttered rye bread. Add ham and cheese.

GRILLED CORNED BEEF SANDWICH

Corned beef, sliced
Sauerkraut
Favorite cheese
Rye bread
Butter

Butter bread on both sides. Place on grill or in frying pan
until one side is done. Remove and put browned side up and

cover with corned beef, then sauerkraut, and top with cheese. Cover with untoasted side out. Return to grill and brown on both sides.

PIMIENTO CHEESE SANDWICH

This recipe is a little more complicated than the others. But it is so delicious that I feel sure you will want to try it some time when you have guests in for bridge.

    ½ lb. sharp cheese, grated
    1 small can pimiento
        Pecans, finely chopped
        Plain mayonnaise to moisten (see recipe below)
    3 egg yolks
    ¼ tsp. salt (scant)
        Dash pepper
    ½ tsp. prepared mustard
    ⅛ cup vinegar
    ¾ cup sugar

Beat egg yolks well. Mix rest of ingredients. Cook until boiled THICK.

Combine plain mayonnaise with cheese, pimiento, and chopped pecans. Blend well. Spread on thin bread.

TOASTED CHEESE SANDWICH

      Cheese to cover slice of bread
    2 thin slices onion
      Mustard to cover inside slices of bread
      Butter

Place cheese and onions between two slices of bread. Butter

outside of slices. Brown on both sides in hot skillet until cheese has melted.

Or: Add two slices of half crisp bacon to sandwich before placing in hot skillet.

GRILLED SWISS CHEESE SANDWICH

   2 slices Swiss cheese
   2 stuffed olives, sliced in six slices
      Hot mustard
      Olive oil for grilling

Spread mustard on inside of two slices of bread. Arrange Swiss cheese on one slice of bread. Add two stuffed olives, sliced. Top with another slice Swiss cheese. Heat in heated olive oil until brown on both sides.

FRIED EGG SANDWICH

      Egg fried on both sides, seasoned to taste
      Slice fried bacon, crisp

Butter toast. Make sandwich by adding egg and bacon.

WESTERN EGG SANDWICH

   1 egg, beaten
   1 TBS. minced onion
   2 TBS. cooked ham, or other meat
   1 TBS. green pepper, diced
   1 TBS. milk
      Salt and ground pepper to taste

Pour all above ingredients into hot skillet. Scramble very slightly until done. Serve between two slices of toast.

EGG SPREAD SANDWICH

2 hard-cooked eggs, mashed
Parsley
Few drops Worcestershire sauce
Pepper to taste
Mayonnaise to moisten

Combine above ingredients. Spread on bread.

TUNA-CHEESETTES

2 oz. processed American cheese, cubed
2 hard-cooked egg yolks, chopped
½ size can tuna, flaked (3½ oz.)
1 TBS. green pepper, chopped
1 TBS. onion, minced
1 TBS. sweet pickle, chopped
4 TBS. salad dressing
1 TBS. stuffed olives, chopped
¼ tsp. salt and pinch pepper
4 hot dog buns

Combine all ingredients, except buns, and mix lightly. Split buns, spread with softened butter, and fill with mixture. Wrap buns in aluminum foil. Place on shallow pan and bake in slow oven (325°) for 35 minutes or until filling is heated.

TUNA SANDWICH

½ size can tuna, flaked (3½ oz.)
2½ TBS. celery, finely chopped

½ TBS. onion, minced
1½ TBS. mayonnaise
½ TBS. lemon juice
¼ tsp. Worcestershire sauce
1 TBS. chopped green pepper
⅛ tsp. ground dill

Combine all ingredients. Spread on bread. Makes several sandwiches.

SHRIMPBURGER

4 fried shrimps (hot) with tails removed
Coleslaw
Hamburger bun, toasted or untoasted

Place shrimp on toasted or untoasted bun. Add coleslaw. Serve immediately.

Or: Instead of coleslaw, use tartar sauce.

SHRIMP SANDWICH

½ cup cooked shrimp, cut in small pieces
1 TBS. butter
4 TBS. celery, diced
½ tsp. lemon juice
French dressing or mayonnaise thinned with milk
Salt and pepper to taste

Combine above ingredients and spread on bread.

SARDINE SANDWICH

Sardines, many as desired
Cream cheese to moisten sardines for spreading
Radishes, chopped and unpeeled

Combine above ingredients. Use on any type bread.

FISH STICK SANDWICH

Fish stick, heated to golden brown
Frankfurter bun, toasted
Pickle relish, catsup, chilli sauce, or mustard

Place fish stick in heated bun. Add spread desired.

CANNED SALMON SANDWICH

Small can salmon, flaked
1/4 cup chopped pickles
1 TBS. lemon juice
Mayonnaise to moisten

Combine ingredients and spread on bread. This will make more than one sandwich.

Or: Add marjoram to taste.

CRAB MEAT SANDWICH

Small can crab meat, flaked
1/2 cup chopped celery
3 TBS. chopped olives
1 tsp. lemon juice

   1 TBS. chopped pimiento
      Mayonnaise to moisten

Combine above ingredients and spread on bread. This will make more than one sandwich.

LIVER SAUSAGE SPREAD

   ¼ lb. liver sausage
   3 TBS. chopped unpeeled cucumber
   ¼ tsp. onion juice
   ¼ tsp. Worcestershire sauce
      Salad dressing to moisten

Mix ingredients together well. Spread on bread.

TURKEY SANDWICH

   ¼ cup ripe olives, cut in small pieces
   ½ cup chopped cooked turkey
   6 TBS. fine chopped celery
   1 TBS. chopped pimiento
   ¼ tsp. salt
  2½ TBS. mayonnaise

Combine all ingredients well. Makes about one cup of filling. Enough for several sandwiches.

CHICKEN SANDWICH

   1 cup diced chicken (or 5½ oz. jar)
      Diced pickles
   ¼ tsp. tarragon

¼ cup chopped green pepper
Mayonnaise to moisten
Salt and ground pepper to taste

Combine all ingredients. Makes about 1½ cups of spread.

OPEN FACE SANDWICH

2 medium-sized tomatoes, sliced
4 slices crisp bacon, cut in half
Sliced cooked chicken
4 sweet gherkins, sliced
Lettuce leaves
Russian dressing (See recipe on page 57)

Arrange above on four slices buttered toast. Cover with Russian dressing.

BANANA-BACON-TOMATO SANDWICH

2 tomato slices
½ banana, cut lengthwise in three slices
2 strips crisp bacon
Mayonnaise

Moisten both bread slices with mayonnaise. Place tomato slices on bottom slice. Add banana slices. Add two strips bacon. Top with remaining slice of bread.

TOASTED OPEN PEANUT BUTTER SANDWICH

Peanut butter
Salt to taste

Spread peanut butter on white bread. Sprinkle with salt. Broil until light brown.

SWEET-NUT SANDWICH

Jelly, jam or preserves
Nuts, chopped

Combine jelly, jam or preserves with nuts. Spread on buttered white bread

CUCUMBER SANDWICH

1 small cucumber, peeled
1 small onion, grated
½ tsp. salad dressing
½ tsp. prepared horse-radish

Peel cucumber. Coarsely grate onion and cucumber. Drain. Mix with horse-radish and salad dressing. Makes about ½ cup of spread.

WATERCRESS SANDWICH

Watercress
Mayonnaise

Spread mayonnaise on both slices of bread. Use watercress as filler.

Or: Add thick bacon, not too crisp, and green onions or chives.

snacks
and dips

You will find that this section of this cookbook has gone a little wild.

Although you live alone—and love it—you probably have your share of parties, or you, with a group of friends, throw many parties.

For that reason these recipes are in full size. One never knows how much party food to prepare— it all seems to depend on the appetites of your guests. When preparing snacks and dips, throw conservatism to the wind and eat to your heart's content.

Most left-over dips can be used as dressing for salads. You will find some of these leftovers very tasty on baked potatoes or used as filling for sandwiches.

PISTACHIO-CHEESE DIP

  1 8-oz. package cream cheese
  3 TBS. crumbled bleu cheese
½ cup light cream
  1 TBS. lemon juice
½ cup chopped salted pistachio nuts

Blend cream cheese and bleu cheese together. Combine with cream. Add lemon juice and nuts. Chill. Makes 1½ cups.

LOBSTER DIP

    1 cup cream sauce
    ⅓ stick butter
    1 small can lobster
    1 TBS. sherry
       Salt to taste
       Dash paprika

Blend all ingredients. Serve as dip or on thin slices white bread.

ONION SOUP DIP

    1 package cream cheese
    1 pint sour cream
    1 package Lipton's Onion Soup Mix

Blend all ingredients until smooth. Add a little more cream if needed. DO NOT ADD SALT.

BLEU CHEESE EGG SPREAD

    1 hard-cooked egg
    2 TBS. bleu cheese
    2 tsp. French dressing

Chop egg very fine. Add bleu cheese and French dressing. Beat until creamy. Tasty spread for crackers or party bread.

SHRIMP SPREAD

1 3 oz. package cream cheese
1 cup boiled or canned shrimp, cut into small pieces
½ tsp. Worcestershire sauce
1 TBS. lemon juice

Blend well cheese, Worcestershire sauce, and lemon juice. Spread on crackers or party bread. If you wish to use for a dip, add mayonnaise to moisten.

SHRIMP HORS D'OEUVRES

1 lb. fresh shrimp, cleaned and cooked
1 TBS. onion, minced
1 tsp. celery, minced
1 tsp. green pepper, minced
2 tsp. lemon juice
½ tsp. grated lemon rind
¼ tsp. salt
4 to 5 drops tabasco sauce
  Dash of pepper
¾ cup mayonnaise

Cut shrimp very fine. Combine with rest of ingredients. Cut about 36 rounds of bread, about the size of a half dollar. Pile heaping teaspoon shrimp mixture on each round of bread. Garnish with parsley. Or this mixture can be used as a dip.

PARTY MIX

⅓ cup Wesson oil
1 TBS. Worcestershire sauce
1 tsp. salt
⅛ tsp. garlic salt or powder
2 cups shredded wheat, bite-size
2 cups shredded rice, bite-size
1½ cups pretzel sticks
½ cup pecan or walnut halves

Heat oven to 300 degrees (slow). Measure Wesson oil. Add Worcestershire sauce, salt, and garlic salt. Beat with fork. Put cereals, pretzel sticks and nuts into 13" x 9" shallow baking pan. Continue beating oil mixture as it is poured over mixture. Stir gently to coat all pieces. Bake 30 minutes, stir every ten minutes. Cool on absorbent paper.

PECAN AND CHEESE HORS D'OEUVRES

16 pecan or walnut halves
½ cup pineapple cheese spread

Make cheese balls of the cheese spread. Press a pecan half on two sides. Chill.

HERRING ON PICKS

½ pint pickled herring
16 small pickled onions

Cut herring into 1" squares. Drain well. Spear an onion, then square of herring and then another onion on an hors d'oeuvre pick.

CRUNCHY SPREAD

  1 cup chopped dried beef
 ½ cup pineapple cheese spread
 ½ cup chopped toasted almonds
  2 TBS. lemon juice
 ⅛″ slices of unpeeled cucumber

Mix first four ingredients. Spread on unpeeled cucumber slices. Do not freeze.

STUFFED CELERY

  2 stalks celery
  6 TBS. butter
  2 oz. cream cheese
    Salt and pepper to taste
    Tomato paste
  6 TBS. bleu cheese

Wash and dry celery well. Cream 3 TBS. butter, cream cheese, salt, and pepper, and color with a little tomato paste. In another bowl cream rest of butter, rub bleu cheese through a strainer. Mix it into butter with a little pepper and *no* salt. Stuff half of celery with bleu cheese mix and other half with cream cheese. Wrap in waxed paper. Cool in refrigerator. Remove, cut into thin slices. Serve on rounds of rye bread.

SHERRIED SHRIMP

 12 cooked shrimp
 ¼ cup minced parsley
  2 hard-cooked eggs

    2 tsp. melted butter
      Salt and pepper to taste
    ¼ cup cream
    ½ cup sherry

Chop hard-cooked eggs and shrimp finely. Mix with parsley, butter, seasoning, and cream. Simmer few minutes. Add sherry. Serve on hot croutons.

RIPE OLIVE CHEESE DIP

    1 3 oz. package cream cheese
    1 cup minced ripe olives
      Dash hot sauce
      Salt and pepper to taste
    ¼ cup cream or mayonnaise

Blend above ingredients. Excellent for either dip or hunks of bread.

WHISKEY BALLS

    30 vanilla wafers, well ground
     2 TBS. cocoa
     2 TBS. white Karo syrup
    ⅓ cup crushed pecans
     4 TBS. bourbon whiskey

Blend all ingredients.
    Make into 1 inch diameter balls. Roll in powdered sugar. You can roll in more crushed pecans if desired.

BARBECUED PECANS

  2 cups pecan halves
  ¾ cup Worcestershire sauce
     Few dashes tabasco sauce
  1 tsp. salt
  3 drops garlic juice, or use garlic powder
  2 TBS. butter

Combine Worcestershire sauce, tabasco, salt, or garlic juice and powder. Heat pecans in heavy skillet with 2 TBS. butter. When well coated, sprinkle 2 TBS. of sauce over nuts. Heat slowly, stirring constantly until absorbed. Gradually add sauce, waiting for it to be absorbed before adding more. This takes about 45 minutes. Nuts will be black and sticky but crisp inside. To store, put in foil lined container and seal.

CHILI CON QUESO DIP AND SPREAD
(Chili with cheese)

  3 slices American type cheese
  4 oz. (½ cup) tomato sauce
  1 diced hot pepper, or amount hot sauce desired

Heat tomato sauce and diced hot pepper or hot sauce. Add cheese torn in bits. Stir over low flame until cheese is melted. Serve over broken, toasted tortillas, corn chips, or as a dip.

CLAM CHEESE DIP

  2 3 oz. packages cream cheese
  1 tsp. lemon juice
  ½ tsp. salt
  1 tsp. Worcestershire sauce

2 TBS. clam liquid
1 clove garlic, finely cut
½ cup minced clams, drained

Mix cream cheese with lemon juice, salt, Worcestershire sauce, clam liquid, and garlic. Add clams. Serve as dip with Frito corn chips.

BACON BITES

Wrap narrow strips of bacon around an assortment of fresh or canned shrimp, pickled onions, and stuffed olives. Secure with toothpicks. Broil until bacon is crisp. Drain off grease Place in chafing dish. Pour in 1 cup of heated rum for each
  2 bites.

SAUSAGES WITH RUM

4 oz. small pork cocktail sausages
½ cup dark brown sugar
½ cup soy bean sauce
½ cup rum

Sauté sausages on one side. Pour out grease. Add sugar and soy bean sauce and turn sausages on other side. Simmer. Place in chafing dish. Add ½ cup heated rum and ignite.

HORSE-RADISH-CHEESE DIP

1 3 oz. package cream cheese
½ cup French dressing
1 tsp. cream style horse-radish
   Few drops Worcestershire sauce
1 tsp. chopped parsley
   arlic if desired

Mash cheese and blend with French dressing. Add other in-gredients. Can also be used for a dip with crisp vegetables.

PEPPY POPCORN

     8 cups salted popped corn
     1 tsp. paprika
    ⅛ tsp. curry powder

Combine paprika and curry powder. Sprinkle over hot popped corn. Stir.

EGGPLANT CAVIAR

     1 eggplant (1 lb. or smaller)
     1 tsp. salad oil
     1 tsp. salt
        Pepper to taste
        Small onion finely chopped
    ½ small green pepper finely chopped
    ½ cup celery very finely chopped
     2 TBS. salad oil
        Hot sauce to taste (optional)

Bake eggplant, greased with 1 tsp. salad oil, wrapped in foil in oven, or on top of stove until well done. Pierce with fork. Peel skin off. Mash pulp well. Add balance of ingredients. Chill. Drain standing liquid. Season again if necessary. Serve as dip or spread for crackers or thin slices of white bread. Can also be used as a dressing for salads.

SARDINE SNACK

     1 can sardines
     1 hard-cooked egg

Parsley
Mayonnaise to soften ingredients well
Salt and pepper to taste
Hot seasonings to taste
Garlic powder

Blend all ingredients well. Serve as spread for crackers or thin slices of white bread. If mixture is very moist, it can also be used as a dip.

BROILED CHICKEN LIVERS

Cook chicken livers in boiling salted water about 20 minutes. Wrap chicken livers with strips of bacon. Pierce with toothpicks. Broil in oven until bacon is done. Serve immediately.

LIVER PÂTÉ

1 lb. calf liver
½ to ¾ cup salad oil
1 large onion diced
4 small hard-cooked eggs
  Salt and pepper to taste

Pan fry liver slowly in cooking oil. Sauté onions until light brown. Grind liver in food grinder with hard-cooked eggs and onion. Add rest of salad oil gradually. Salt and pepper to taste. Serve as a spread on crackers or thin slices of rye bread. Can also be served as a side dish.

AVOCADO DIP

1 3 oz. package cream cheese
1 ripe avocado, medium size

1 tsp. lemon juice
Salt
2 TBS. mayonnaise
1 TBS. milk

Mash avocado well. Blend with rest of ingredients. Serve as a dip or cracker or bread spread. Can also be used as dressing for a salad.

AVOCADO-CHILI DIP

Avocado
Lemon juice
Chili powder
Tomato, finely diced
Salt to taste
Ground pepper to taste

Mash avocado and enough lemon juice to moisten. Add as much chili powder as you desire. Combine well. Add diced tomato, salt and pepper. Very good served as dip for raw vegetables, potato chips or crackers.

FRESH GRAPEFRUIT DIP

4 oz. cream cheese
8 drops tabasco
½ tsp. Worcestershire sauce
1½ tsp. lemon juice
½ grapefruit
Paprika
Chopped parsley

Mix cheese, seasonings, and lemon juice until fluffy. Remove grapefruit sections and cut into small pieces. Add fruit and juice to cheese mixture. Spoon into grapefruit shell. Garnish with paprika and parsley.

SKINLESS WEENIE HORS D'OEUVRES

1½ doz. skinless weenies
  3 cups vinegar
  ⌐ cup water
  1 lemon sliced
  2 small onions sliced
  1 large or 2 medium sour pickles, sliced
    Several small green hot peppers
    Several cloves garlic
  2 tsp. pickling spices

Boil weenies in water for 30 minutes. Drain. Pack in jars with lemon, onion, and pickles. Mix water, vinegar, peppers, garlic, and pickling spice. Boil. Pour over weenies and seal. Let stand week to ten days preferably in refrigerator. As used, slice crosswise in ¼″ slices, stab each slice with a toothpick.

CELERY SEED DIP

  1 package cream cheese
  1 tsp. celery seed
  ¼ cup cream or mayonnaise
    Paprika
    Tabasco to taste

Blend all of ingredients. Serve as dip or spread on rounds of canape toast.

ANCHOVY DIP

¼ cup French dressing
1 8-oz. pkg. cream cheese
1 TBS. Worcestershire sauce
1 TBS. grated onion
1 TBS. anchovy paste

Gradually add French dressing to cream cheese. Blend well. Add rest of ingredients, mixing well.

WEENIES IN BLANKET

1 can weenies
1 can frozen biscuits
  Mustard
  Parsley

Flatten biscuits and place whole or part of weenie in center. Add mustard and sprinkle little parsley on top. Fold over to cover completely. Sprinkle parsley on top. Cut in two. Follow baking directions on biscuit package or bake until brown.

Or: Dehydrated onion may be sprinkled on top of weenies.

OLIVE CHEESE BITES

1 egg
1 TBS. milk
½ tsp. Worcestershire sauce
  Salt to taste
  Dash tabasco sauce
2 cups grated American cheese (not packed)
9 slices bread

5 slices bacon
½ cup chopped ripe olives

Beat egg with milk and seasonings. Blend in cheese. Add
more milk if needed to spread more easily. Trim crusts from
bread. Toast one side under broiler. Cover untoasted side
with olives, spread with cheese, and cut bread into quarters.
Top each piece with one 1 inch strip of bacon. Broil until
brown. Makes 3 dozen.

SALMON PICK-UPS

1 can (7 to 8 oz.) salmon, drained and flaked
1 pkg. (3 oz.) cream cheese, softened
2 TBS. sour cream
2 TBS. chopped green olives
1 TBS.sgrated onion
¼ tsp. salt
Pepper to taste

Combine all ingredients. Chill. Shape into half-inch balls.
Roll in minced parsley or chives, if desired. Chill again. Serve
n toothpicks. Make 3

Or. S read mixture on thi cucumber slices. Chill.

SPICED CHEESE DIP

8 oz. cheese slices (Muenster, sharp, or American)
1 tsp. garlic juice
1 TBS. horse-radish
1 tsp. prepared mustard
1 tsp. Worcestershire sauce
¼ tsp. tabasco
1 tsp. soy sauce

¼ tsp. caraway seed
½ tsp. chives
   Light cream

Put cheese with soy sauce through a food grinder. Add remaining ingredients while beating with a wooden spoon. At the same time, add cream gradually until the mixture is smooth. DO NOT CHILL. Use on hot potato chips for dunking.

 # mexican food

No true Texan would dare to write a cookbook unless it included a section on Mexican foods, Texas style. Summer or winter, we get a craving for Mexican food. Displaced Texans in the United States or abroad are always searching for Mexican food. Many a fond mother ships canned Mexican food to her children when they are living in foreign countries. To a displaced Texan, finding canned tortillas is like finding a bank error in your favor. So, for those of you who are wondering what we have been talking about—and for those of you who have been looking for Mexican food recipes —have fun eating!

CHILI CON CARNE

- ½ lb. ground meat in bite-size chunks, or beef finely cut
- 1½ to 2 TBS. Gebhardt's Chili Powder or Chili-Quik
- 1 clove garlic, minced
- 2 TBS. fat
- ½ tsp. salt
- 1 cup water
- 1 medium sized onion, chopped

Simmer meat and onions until slightly brown. Dilute water with Chili Powder or Chili-Quik. Put meat, onions, and garlic in saucepan. Simmer slowly for 45 minutes to 1 hour. Chili can be re-heated quickly when ready to eat.

CHILI BEANS (See page 92).

TACOS

Tortillas
Chopped cooked beef
Shredded lettuce and tomato finely chopped
Hot sauce

Dip tortillas for just a minute in hot grease so they will fold without breaking. Lay tortilla flat, fill with bit of ground meat, shredded lettuce and tomato. Fasten with toothpick so it will hold together.

MASHED FRIJOLES (Mashed Beans)

Mash beans, following chili beans recipe, page 92. Roll into small flat balls. Fry like potato patties.

ENCHILADAS

Make chili con carne, page 166. Prepare chili beans, page 92. For each tortilla, ½ TBS. grated American cheese, and 1 tsp. minced onion.

Dip each tortilla in hot grease for second to keep tortilla from breaking when folding. On each tortilla, spoon 1 TBS. chili con carne, 1 tsp. chili beans, sprinkle cheese, and onion. Fold over and fasten with one or two toothpicks. Put in baking dish, size to depend on how many enchiladas you are preparing. After laying tortillas in dish, add more chili con carne and chili beans on top. Grate a lot of cheese over top and add onions as desired. Place in hot oven until cheese melts. Serve on hot platter.

CHILI CON QUESO Chili with Cheese (See Page 157)

MEXICAN RICF (See Page 108)

SPANISH RICE

Follow recipe on pre-cooked rice box.
Instead of using canned tomatoes, substitute catsup or tomato juice.

CUACAMOLE SALAD (See Page 45)

ONE MEAL FRITO CHILI PIE CASSEROLE

⅔ cup chili
1 cup Fritos corn chips
½ onion, chopped
⅓ cup grated American cheese

Place ⅔ cup Fritos in small baking dish. Arrange chopped onions and half of grated cheese over Fritos. Pour heated chili over onions and cheese. Top with remaining Fritos and grated cheese. Bake at 350 degrees for 10 minutes.

TOASTED TORTILLAS

Put cooking oil on one side of tortillas. Toast in flat pan. Turn over.

Or: After turning tortilla over, sprinkle with cheese and chopped chives or chopped onion tops. Toast until cheese is melted.

MEXICAN CANDY (PRALINES) (See Page 128)

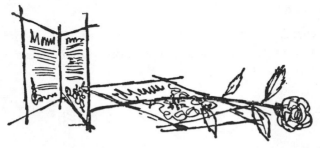

suggested menus

A properly fed person is a happy person. When you have trouble "making yourself eat," try variety in your meals. Try out new recipes. Even if you don't like them it will be a change. You may already be familiar with some of these suggested menus—others may brighten your eating outlook. It's fun to experiment!

Paprika-Mustard Fried Chicken (Page 82)
Mint Peas (Page 93)
Italian Salad (Page 48)
Coffee Chiffon Cake (Page 117)

Fish Croquettes (Page 87)
Kidney Beans (Page 91)
Tomato and Cucumber Salad with Garlic Dressing (Page 51)
Chocolate Pecan Squares (Page 122)

Enchiladas (Page 167)
Mexican Rice (Page 108)

Avocado Salad
Toasted Tortillas (Page 169)
Mexican Candy (Pralines) (Page 128)

Steak (Page 67 or Fry Pan Cooking Chart)
Baked Potato (Page 96)
Salad with Herb Marinade Dressing (Page 56)
Peppermint Ice-Cream Cake (Page 115)

Tuna-Chessettes (Page 145)
Apple and Grapefruit Salad (Page 49)
Butterscotch Peach Crisp (Page 111)

Individual Meat and Noodle Dish (Page 71)
Cottage Cheese and Tomato Salad
Carrot Bread (Page 140)

Italian Broiled Shrimp (Page 88)
Wild Rice (Page 108)
Toasted Sesame Seed Salad (Page 49)
Angel Food Pie (Page 124)

Thyme and Wine Chicken (Page 84)
String Beans (Page 92)
Potato Salad (Page 44)
Drop Tea Cakes (Page 122)

Barbecued Frankfurters (Page 73)
Pork and Beans with Parsley
Tossed Salad with dressing
Cocoa Cake (Page 116)

Curried Crab (Page 90)
Baked Tomato (Page 97)

Banana and Cabbage Salad
Baked Lemon Pudding (Page 113)

Hamburger (Page 141)
French Fried Onions (Page 95)
Strawberry Frost (Page 112)

Grilled Corned Beef Sandwich (Page 142)
Casserole Squash (Page 94)
Poppy Seed Cake (Page 118)

Meat Loaf (Page 70)
Parsley potatoes baked with meat loaf
Pineapple cream cheese salad (Page 50)
Baked Apples (Page 110)

Lobster Salad (Page 47)
Stuffed Hard-Cooked eggs (Page 40)
Strawberry Shortcake (Page 119)

PARTY BUFFET FOR THE BUDGET-MINDED

Eggplant Caviar (Page 159)
Sardine Snack (Page 159)
Liver Pâté (Page 160)
Chili Con Queso Dip (Page 157)
Avocado Dip (Page 160)
Party bread, or Rye party bread sliced very, very thin
Fritos
Potato chips
Cheeses sliced thin and small enough to place on party bread
Pickles sliced thin
Small tomatoes, sliced very thin
Tequila Salty Dogs (Page 131)

index

[173]